2021: My Last Hope

Book 4 of 5

Douglas Schnapp

ISBN: 979-8-9891218-7-8

And Like That, He's Gone

"Where are you?"

A valid question. People asked Ensign that question more often than any other. Ensign ignored it. He had other things on his mind. Ensign spoke into his phone as if in his own world.

"You know something? I'll do crystal for the rest of my life."

He was thinking aloud. Previous addictions always ended. Ensign couldn't find a single reason to stop using methamphetamine. Over the past few years, the benefits of constant crystal consumption easily outweighed the downsides of around-the-clock indulgence in his chemically altered mind.

On crystal, Ensign had no desire to use any other substances. He had more energy; sleeping three hours every two days also gave him much more time. Ensign stayed busy; his creativity was expressed through work on various projects at every given moment. He connected sexually; intimacy was prolonged and more meaningful. Ensign was outgoing; fear and anxiety were easily overcome. Ensign felt alive; he sought out others to share his world…if only for isolated fleeting moments.

The drugs allowed Ensign to maintain all those interactions and meetings; drugs moved him through the world of adult social media popularity at an accelerated pace. He took more risks which led to more new and unique experiences. Ensign saw the benefits of methamphetamine in all aspects of his life. The drugs gave him perspective through crystal-colored glasses. An endless supply of the highest grade; Ensign never worried about running out of drugs. The money from crystal kept Ensign going in times of need.

Though he was content with remaining an indefinite user of methamphetamine, Ensign was again working towards freeing himself from the game. Ensign was homeless, but the entire country was his home. It was a trade-off he happily accepted. Ensign relished the effects of continuous indulgence. The drugs sheltered his mind from any negative side effects of those same drugs.

Much has been seen from the media regarding the stigma of drug addiction. All other drugs had been those detriments; the familiar problems stated in news reports and studies. Crystal was different. Ensign had seen lives ruined by methamphetamine, in the media and in person. Ensign didn't respond to crystal in all those negative ways like the others. He knew he had a golden ticket; he had a pass. He didn't want for the drug; he didn't struggle without it. While high, Ensign looked past the fact that his life had been turned completely upside down.

Ensign had privilege, one which kept him from ever knowing a day of wishing to get high without the means to do so. That part of the crystal meth scene didn't exist in Ensign's world. His view was skewed. Ensign's world, from his viewpoint, was full steam ahead...but it wasn't steam; it was smoke. There was so much smoke; Ensign couldn't see past the cloud in front of him.

It was the dawn of 2021, and Ensign jumped into the year; he was full of excitement and wonder. He didn't know. He couldn't have known. Had he known, things would have been different. Of course they would have, but life wasn't about knowing the outcome. Everyone's just along for the ride...right?

Here We Go

Ensign hung up the phone. As he drove, he thought about his stop that morning in Arlington, Ohio. That look on his dad's face when Ensign walked in; was it disappointment? Yes…it was disappointment for sure. Something else was there as well. Ensign smiled when he first stepped into the gunsmithing shop on his dad's property. When Ensign's father looked up at him, he didn't smile back. Ensign saw the recognition register, and that next look caused Ensign's heart to sink. After six years without contact, the look on Ensign's dad's face made Ensign rethink his decision to stop by and see him. He pushed past it. Ensign greeted his father…

Ensign shook the memory of that morning from his head. In that moment, he had other concerns. It was dark outside. Ensign approached the bottom of Ohio on southbound I-75. Late evening traffic, north of Cincinnati, had been growing denser by the minute. The Subaru camper/car had begun to experience electrical issues on the drive. Ensign had already stopped outside of Dayton to try to sort out the issues with the car's wiring. With the wiring in check, the signs pointed to the alternator.

Then, as with his previous cars on previous cross-country trips, the Subaru simply shut off. No engine, no headlights, no power steering, no anything. Ensign was on the busy freeway, and he was careening through traffic at seventy miles an hour in a rolling camper/car with no power. Unlike previous car failures, Ensign and his camper/car had an out. There was an exit ramp up on the right. Ensign saw the ramp, and he also noticed that the exit instantly became a slope downward from the elevated freeway.

The exit was reachable, even considering current catastrophic camper/car conditions. Though he needed to cut across three lanes to the right, there was a gap in the traffic around him. Ensign pulled the wheel hard, using muscle in place of the inoperable power steering. He reached the ramp. As he coasted down the hill, Ensign continued at highway speed. There was one car, far ahead of him, at the bottom of the ramp. Ensign hoped the car would make it to the intersection before the green light changed to red at the bottom of the hill. The light changed to yellow. The car ahead of Ensign could have easily made the light...

"Keep going! Keep going! Keep going! No!"

Ensign stomped his foot down on the brake pedal. His Subaru camper/car slowed down to stop behind the other car at the very bottom of the hill. Just after the three cars in cross-traffic began to fill the intersection in front of him, the light quickly turned green again. The car in front of Ensign took off into the night. Ensign stepped from his car and began to push. There was no longer momentum from descending the hill. Ensign had to start from scratch. The road was flat. With much effort, he pushed his car through the intersection and down the street on the other side.

As Ensign struggled, a car pulled up next to him. The driver offered his help. Ensign climbed back into his driver's seat, and the other car lined up behind Ensign's Subaru. The other car pushed Ensign half a mile down the road to the first and only available parking lot.

"Thank you for your help. You're a lifesaver."

"Yeah, man; no problem. Be careful out here tonight. This isn't a good part of town."

Ensign watched; that other car disappeared down the road and into the night. He took a deep breath, and he evaluated his situation. Ensign was in a bank parking lot. There was nothing else around. Ensign was alone in the Cincinnati darkness. He could hear the cars passing a few hundred yards away on the interstate above him. The surface streets were empty. Random streetlights illuminated the dark Cincinnati sky.

Ensign shook his head. His cross-country trip from Michigan to Florida; already a multitude of difficulties and complications were testing him. Still north of Ohio's border with Kentucky, Ensign had a long way to go. Had he been driving in a functional car on the highway, he would have been ten minutes from crossing over the Ohio River. A functional car was no longer part of Ensign's reality. In the blink of a headlight, Ensign's reality had become an ordeal.

Alone in the Night

One o'clock in the morning; it was one o'clock in the morning. Ensign listened to the reply; the tow truck driver was confident in his answer. Ensign ignored the confidence and asked again.

"Are you sure? Well, I'll be here. I have no other option."

"Yes, I'll reach the shop in Kentucky at five thirty. I'll be up to you in Ohio just after six. Hang tight and try to stay warm. Be careful. I know that part of town. It definitely isn't where you want to be stranded."

That was the second warning about safety in that location. Ensign just shook his head as he hung up the phone. Since sleep in the wintry night wasn't going to be possible, drugs were on the schedule for the duration. Drugs would have been on the schedule regardless, but it was time to go above and beyond. With the shades up in the windows, the torch ignited, and the lines dumped out on the silver serving tray, it was time to get to work. How much crystal would it take to override the stress of the night? It was time Ensign found out.

There was too much smoke. After a half hour, Ensign had to open the doors and step from the car for some fresh air. The clouds flowed from the car doors and dissipated into the brisk night air. The winter wind instantly chilled the sweat covering Ensign's body. There was a sound in the distance. It was music: bass. The distant thumps slowly grew louder as Ensign let the last of the drug smoke out of the car. Ensign had to make a decision. Where was he going to be when the car with the loud bass reached him? He thought on it for a split second. He was going to be inside his car with the shades covering all the windows.

The volume increased as the car blatantly headed in Ensign's direction. Ensign sat back and peered through a crack alongside the shade in one of his car's windows. The car, blacked out with dark window tint, stopped moving; it idled on a street across from the parking lot where Ensign was camping. The music cut off. As the car inched forward, the driver adjusted position to directly face Ensign's Subaru. Headlights illuminated Ensign's vehicle in the dark Cincinnati night. Five minutes passed, and Ensign adjusted his grip on his handgun.

The car began to drive; not in the direction it had been heading, but it turned to pull into the parking lot. Ensign's Subaru was parked directly in the middle of the lot. The other car, still without music, slowly circled the lot around Ensign like a shark circling its prey in the ocean. Ensign sat still inside his vehicle. The other car circled three times. Ensign watched through the cracks on the sides of the window shades. Out of nowhere, the other car suddenly left the lot and disappeared down a street, into the night.

Ensign kept his gun in his hand. He made sure all of his drug paraphernalia was secured out of sight. The loud bass thumped again as the other car drove away. Ensign listened as the beats faded off. Time passed. It was hard to stay warm. The side effects of crystal on Ensign's circulatory system caused his fingers and toes to ache in the cold. Ensign continued to keep a vigilant ear to listen for approaching people and vehicles. The night was silent. It was eerie.

Two hours passed. Ensign froze. Was it the same car as before? Ensign again stashed his drugs. He continued to listen intently as the faint sound of bass notes floated to him in the darkness. Again, the music slowly grew louder. Whether it was the same car or a different car, it was for sure getting closer. It was again decision time. Ensign decided to act. He strapped his gun around his upper arm, and he pulled the lever to pop the hood. With his gun blatantly visible around his left arm, Ensign grabbed a screwdriver and began to work on the wiring to the alternator of the Subaru.

Ensign heard the car as it reached the same cross street where that earlier car had previously stopped. The hood of the Subaru blocked vision between Ensign and the emergent vehicle. Ensign stood up from the front of the engine compartment and walked around towards the back of the Subaru to get a look at who was approaching. It was the same car as before, windows completely blacked out.

Ensign held a steady gaze towards the windshield of the car a hundred yards in front of him. As it had earlier, the car's music cut off. As casually as possible, Ensign opened the back door to the Subaru. He tossed the screwdriver into the back, and he pulled out a metric socket wrench. As Ensign turned to walk back to the engine compartment to tighten the bolts on his car's alternator, the car with the tinted windows peeled out and turned down a side street. Ensign heard the music kicking back on as the car's engine roared. Both the engine and the music again faded out into the night. That was the last time that Ensign saw the car with the blacked-out windows.

At five fifteen, the phone rang. The tow truck driver was running ahead of schedule. He was leaving the shop in Kentucky. At five forty-five, Ensign watched the tow truck pull into the parking lot. After securing his drugs in his backpack, Ensign stepped out of his car to meet the driver. The two of them hooked the Subaru to the cables, and Ensign steered his car as it was pulled up onto the bed of the truck by the tow winch.

It was still dark, and the interstate through Cincinnati was void of almost all traffic. Soon, they were across the Ohio River and in Kentucky. Ensign used his phone to find a location of an auto supply store in Kentucky. After another half hour, the Subaru was safely unloaded into a parking space in front of the store. When the tow truck was out of sight, Ensign took the drugs out of his backpack and did a couple hotrails.

Get in the Zone

Ensign's physiology was in tune with his drug regimen. His body and mind were conditioned and fully accustomed to methamphetamine. Though crystal generally reduced appetite, Ensign was at a homeostasis. He ate food on a regular schedule. He was also able to do substantial amounts of drugs and fall asleep, especially when he had been awake a while. As the sky lightened from black to a dark purple that morning, Ensign put away his drug equipment and went to sleep in the bed in his Subaru camper/car. The Sun was about to rise, and Ensign wanted to sleep a few hours before the auto supply store opened.

It was mid-morning when Ensign woke up. Other cars were parked in various spaces in the store's parking lot. Ensign went into the store and asked about the alternator he needed to buy for his car. There wasn't the needed alternator in stock at the store. The clerk made a phone call. A store on the other side of the city had one in stock. Luckily for Ensign, one of the store employees was about to make a trip to pick up parts from the other store. With the alternator added to the list, Ensign went back out to his car to do drugs and wait.

Ensign sat in the driver's seat of the Subaru. For some reason, paranoia was bad that morning. Ensign kept thinking that random customers were aware of his drug use. A lady walked into the store. Through the glass storefront windows, Ensign saw her walk up to the register and begin speaking to a clerk. Ensign immediately packed up his drug equipment and decided to sit on the curb in plain view for the rest of his waiting time. The drugs were locked in the car, and Ensign felt some relief from the paranoia.

Halfway through changing out his alternator with the new one later that morning, a police cruiser pulled up and parked two spaces over from Ensign. The paranoia came back in a wave which washed over him. Ensign remained on task, but he watched the officer walk into the store and stand by the door to speak with the clerk. The officer stayed at the store for the remainder of the time Ensign spent changing alternators. With shaky hands, Ensign finally finished the job. Ensign walked back into the store to thank the clerk for his help. He bid the clerk and the officer a good day, and he immediately drove from the auto supply store's parking lot.

Ensign kept his eyes on his mirrors, but the police car never pulled out behind him. The paranoia, still with him, had him hurriedly driving away. Ensign didn't take any extra time to look up directions back to the interstate; he just sped down roads in the directions he assumed would lead him to the highway. After stressfully careening through the surface streets, Ensign's paranoia was finally left behind when he found an onramp to the interstate. There were no police behind him, and Ensign was back on track to Florida.

Back on track...for one hour. One hour of driving on the interstate; that was all Ensign managed. On an overpass in dense afternoon traffic, Ensign's fuel pump went out. He couldn't believe it; broken down again, and he was still only in northern Kentucky. Cars honked as they ripped past the Subaru while Ensign was stopped on the narrow right shoulder atop an overpass. With each honk, Ensign's frustration grew. Horn honks were met with middle fingers; all in vain. More time passed. The next tow truck finally arrived.

It was dark outside again when Ensign's Subaru was dropped down into a parking space in the back row of a truck stop parking lot. Ensign made sure his car was set down into a parking space as much out of the way as possible. He knew he was going to be there for some time. The truck stop/travel center was large. There were many spaces in the parking lot. The truck stop/travel center was busy. Many of the spaces were occupied with vehicles.

Coming from a background in transportation and logistics, Ensign had an advantage. Having traveled the country many times over on his perpetual road trip, Ensign felt comfortable in the setting where he had been placed. He was parked amongst a row of personal vehicles belonging to long-haul truck drivers. The cars were there to remain as the truck drivers were out on the road working. Ensign knew the cars would sit for up to a couple of weeks at a time while the drivers hauled freight around the country. Though he was stranded, Ensign was content with his car's position, secure in the parking space at the rest stop.

Ensign's first order of business that evening at the Kentucky truck stop: add on to the already ridiculous hotrail stem he used for drugs. Hotrail stems were straight glass tubes. Once they were heated too many times with a torch, the stems cracked and broke off at the ends when overheated. Ensign had been taking the broken stems and connecting them together into one huge pipe back when he was still in the garage in Michigan; his temporary home where he worked to make his Subaru into a camper at the end of 2020. His thoughts: the bigger the stem, the more crystal he could scrape from the inside of the glass. Scraping crystal was oddly satisfying. The hotrails of crystal residue got him just as high as first-pass crystal.

The pipe was made from broken pieces, added together as glass stems broke from heating them. The pipe approached two feet in length. Epoxy, colored electrical wiring, and hot glue held the pieces together. Since only the end of the pipe was heated to do hotrails, the other substances beyond the glass ends weren't subjected to the torch. Ensign made sure the stem on the end of the pipe was still long enough to be cool where the binding items held the pipe together at the start of the next stem. Ensign painted a colorful spiral design around the outside of the pipe using his tattoo ink. Clear epoxy resin covered the length of the ink design, protecting it in a clear coating.

Crystal had that effect on Ensign; he was always busy doing and creating anything that swirled into his head. He moved from task to task, creation to creation. As his mind swirled with thoughts, his work was never done. Car work, car audio work, tattooing, documenting, creating media, interacting online with people all over, sharing intimacy, random projects popped up all the time...

That Frankenpipe wasn't Ensign's first order of business that evening. He had been distracted when he pulled Frankenpipe from its secure hiding space within the dismantled dashboard of the Subaru. As Ensign did drugs, the colorful spiral of the pipe mesmerized him. He had another broken pipe to add to his glass monstrosity. In that moment, he was consumed with pipe dreams.

A minute after blowing out the last cloud, Ensign remembered what he actually needed to do before anything else. Ensign put the giant pipe away, and his brain began to properly prioritize his task list. He needed to get online and order a new fuel pump. He found one and placed the order...to the parking lot of the random Kentucky truck stop. In the shipping notes, Ensign described his car and parking space location. There was no next-day delivery. The fuel pump wasn't going to arrive over the upcoming weekend. Delivery was set, and the fuel pump was scheduled to arrive the Friday of the following week.

There was a Denny's restaurant connected to the travel center at the truck stop. Ensign knew he was about to consume more southwest skillet breakfasts than he had in all the time in his life leading up to that point. There were showers at the truck stop. There were all the amenities needed for over a week's worth of parking lot camping. People were everywhere inside and outside the bustling service center. Ensign settled in, and he got to work; extending his hotrail pipe another few inches.

Four Score and Six

Was that the phone ringing? Ensign tried to shake off the fog from only an hour of sleep. He was dropped off at his car earlier that morning by a lady he met on the internet. The prior night was spent at the lady's house. That hour of sleep that morning was his first sleep in two days. The fog began to lift. It was, in fact, Ensign's phone ringing. Ensign knew he needed to answer it. Projected delivery of the new fuel pump was that morning. Ensign searched around him in his camper/car to locate his phone before the ringing stopped.

The phone went silent. Ensign found it a moment later. It wasn't a call from the delivery, but there was a message he had missed. Ensign fully woke up as he read the message, more bad news. The message was regarding the delivery of the fuel pump, and Ensign hadn't been awake to reply in a timely manner. Ensign's trip to Florida was becoming more and more challenging, and he was only two states further than where he had started.

"We attempted to deliver your package, but we were unable to complete the delivery."

The remainder of the day was spent on the phone. Ensign did drugs in his car in the parking lot at the rest stop in Kentucky while he tried to sort out the situation. The delivery driver, according to customer service, wasn't comfortable delivering to a car in a parking lot. According to customer service: without an address, the delivery would not be able to be completed.

Ensign, feeling dejected, wondered what the future held for him. The year was off to a shaky start. Before the dark of night set in, Ensign made sure that the top of his fuel tank was securely bolted back into place. He didn't want to accidentally blow himself up while doing hotrails in the camper/car. With nothing else to look forward to that day, Ensign got a full night of much needed sleep.

After eating food from Denny's the following morning, a random thought entered Ensign's head. He dressed and headed into the service center. Ensign walked up to a cash register and asked the clerk a question.

"Hi. My name's Ensign. I was supposed to receive a delivery yesterday. It's a part for my car. Did you guys happen to get a package with my name on it?"

"I'm not sure. Let me get the manager and see if he knows anything."

Ensign's heart raced as he waited to speak with the manager. The service center, as it had been each day he was there, was extremely busy. Ten minutes passed as adrenaline mixed with the meth in Ensign's body. Though he was told the delivery couldn't be completed, Ensign had a feeling of hope that morning. Sure enough, after showing his driver's license to the manager of the service center, Ensign walked back out to his Subaru with a new fuel pump in his hands.

A week and a half; a week and a half of winter camping in a broken-down car at a rest stop in Kentucky, and Ensign saw an end in sight. Having previously removed the old fuel pump, installing the new fuel pump was a fast process. The moment of truth was upon him. Ensign bolted the cover back onto the fuel tank. He left his tools out in case the installation wasn't successful.

As he sat in the driver's seat of his car, Ensign's mind was all over the place. Before trying to start his car, Ensign pulled out his two-foot long Frankenpipe and blew down a couple large hotrails of crystal. He was ready. Hope was with him. He was about to find out if luck was on his side. Ensign stuck the key in the Subaru's ignition. He took a deep breath, and he turned the key.

"Yes!"

First try, the engine turned over and the car started. Relief washed over Ensign's drug-saturated brain. Ensign removed the shades from the windows of his car, and he put his tools away. He was ready to get back on the road. Ensign wondered if good fortune was finally on his side. Though he had a reprieve for the moment, good fortune was not on his side.

He didn't know it at the time, but the real car problems on that drive were still a few hours away. Ensign had an easy time while safe at that rest stop. He had been parked in a safe location with access to food and amenities. He had a working phone in an area with phone service. He had a warm service station when the cold February nights became too much to handle. In retrospect, Ensign's time at that rest stop was a cake walk. All of that was about to drastically change. Life was about to hit hard. Ensign wasn't prepared…

Lifelong Midlife Crisis

2021 began with difficulty. 2021; perseverance in the face of adversity. Life; a series of ups and downs. Back in 2018, the downs culminated at a point where Ensign couldn't continue. He made that deal, the deal with himself, as a final effort to find some purpose and meaning in an emptiness which he felt in all he did. Everything changed in 2018...or did it? Outside circumstances absolutely did change in many ways, but Ensign was still the same. Ensign chose to leave his life and explore the unfamiliar. Those outside changes: no career, no home, no familiarity...it was as if he made life harder on purpose. Ensign wanted to feel alive. In his new life, Ensign was forced to act constantly to progress forward. Though he progressed, he had no clear goals.

That deal with himself; Ensign would keep going until he had at least authored a book. There were no steps and no structure in place to reach that goal. Ensign had essentially given himself new obstacles and struggles in immediate ways; ways which distracted him from his unhappiness. As with previous relationships and substance abuse, immediacy served to cloud his view of his actual mental state. Ensign had sabotaged himself. He had set himself up for failure, though he chose to view it as a new and exciting way to live. Perspective.

For three years, Ensign got by on momentum. The online adult hookup world had been good to him. The illicit substance market, though stressful, had allowed him through. Ensign coasted as he watched life unfold around him. As the remnants of his previous life gradually wore off, reality began to creep into Ensign's world. As Ensign took steps away from his means, he hadn't prepared for the next steps in his life. By 2021, logical progression was no longer an upward trajectory.

The factors from Ensign's previous world began to wear thin; the stability of permanent residency and lifelong relationships faded into the background. Stability; washed away to nothing with the memories of ghosts…the echoes of that phrase; more distinct and frequent in Ensign's mind as the factors of that sentiment pushed more into the background and away from Ensign's current being. Washed away to nothing with the memories of ghosts; as Ensign separated from his past, he was washing away from a life which once contained him.

That perfect storm of both internal and external events which culminated in Ensign's departure from current reality back in 2018 had reached its peak in the beginning of 2021. The ascent from that cliff's edge which allowed Ensign to rocket forward and upward for three years had reached a saddle point as 2021 began. There was a new perfect storm; one which had been brewing on a countdown since that initial break three years prior. Trajectory, no longer linear and upward, was set to complicate everything in Ensign's world. 2021; the hardest of the forty-one years of Ensign's existence, had begun. 2021 had begun rough, and trajectory was headed downward to points previously unknown.

Two hours on the southbound interstate in Kentucky, and the alternator began to act up. Ensign knew it was about to go out. It had happened to him before in a different car. Ensign had learned of the faulty line of alternators coming from the particular auto parts chain store after changing out three alternators in a row back in 2018. He didn't have any other options when he was towed from Ohio to Kentucky two weeks earlier.

Though the alternator was failing, Ensign's new fuel pump was working fine. After searching online for the closest particular auto store to exchange the alternator, Ensign plugged the directions into his phone. He needed to make it another forty-five minutes south to reach the store. Having had the issue before, Ensign didn't stress over the situation.

Ensign took out his alternator, and he returned it to the store. To avoid a repeat of the issue, he walked across the street to a different auto supply chain store and purchased another alternator. Ensign walked back to his car in the parking lot of the first store. Ensign did a hotrail, and then he quickly installed the new alternator in his Subaru. He was back on the road in under an hour, crisis avoided.

Hours later, Ensign was on the interstate in the dark of night, approaching southern Kentucky. Though the alternator was fine, an unforeseen problem arose due to the previous faulty alternator. As Ensign reached a split at the top of an overpass where two interstate highways intersected, in the middle lane, in semi-heavy highway traffic, and still on a steep incline... the new battery died: damaged from the issues with the faulty alternator.

And like that; Ensign's real problems began. If only he could have been back at that comfortable rest stop in northern Kentucky where he spent the majority of the previous two weeks. That rest stop: where just that morning he had done everything in his power to vacate it and leave it behind. Ensign had it good at that rest stop. Life was easy. He had taken it for granted.

Ensign's car came to a stop in the middle of the interstate split. He immediately put his car in park. He set his parking brake to prevent his Subaru from rolling backward, down the hill behind him, into oncoming highway traffic. There were three lanes of traffic splitting off to his passenger side and onto the overpass to his right. Two more lanes split to the left of him, beyond his driver's side, and onto the overpass of the other highway.

Ensign was a few hundred feet from the apex of the split. Traffic zoomed by him on both sides; horns honking as cars passed. He had no power. He couldn't even use the four-way hazard lights in the dark night sky. Trucks, flying by him at seventy miles per hour, shook Ensign's car with their proximity.

Ensign was in immediate danger. He needed a plan, and he needed to move fast.

Ensign thought for a moment as he did drugs in his car. He knew what he had to do. He set his phone in the holder hanging from his windshield, and he began recording video. Ensign had to pick his moment carefully. The truck traffic was particularly heavy at the split. Any false move could easily result in death. Ensign watched the groups of cars and trucks as they quickly approached the split and veered off to the two interstates on either side of him. He saw the gap in the distance behind him. Ensign waited in anticipation; his moment came. Suddenly, it was time.

With a small gap in the traffic almost to him, Ensign lowered the parking break and put his car in neutral. He adjusted the steering wheel. When the last car passed by his driver's side door, Ensign jumped out onto the pavement beside his car. He gripped the steering wheel with one hand and pushed the door frame of his car with all his might. As the Subaru began to roll backwards down the hill, toward the next group of vehicles of oncoming traffic, Ensign jumped back in his car.

Ensign muscled the steering wheel the best he could as he sat in his seat; turned to face out the back windshield to watch where his car was rolling. The Subaru began to pick up speed as it rolled backward down the hill. The next group of oncoming traffic was approaching. The headlights in the distance grew brighter. Ensign pulled hard on the wheel, and the Subaru cut across the three lanes of traffic: to the shoulder on the right side of the overpass.

Ensign's Subaru reached the shoulder halfway down the hill. Just as all of his wheels cleared the line which marked the shoulder, the next group of oncoming traffic reached the overpass split. As Ensign applied the brakes and his car rolled to a stop on the shoulder, the horn from a passing semi hurt his ears. His car vibrated from the closeness of the encounter. Ensign had managed to roll his car backwards down a hill on an interstate into oncoming traffic without being smashed to bits.

Ensign was safe on the shoulder of the highway as long as cars remained in their travel lanes as they drove by. The most immediate concern that night had been managed. It was then that Ensign began to realize all of the other concerns he faced. Ensign took another moment to do drugs while he watched the video which he recorded of pushing his car to safety. He then took a moment to evaluate all the latest problems in his world.

There was no phone service.

Ensign was in the middle of nowhere, which meant he had nowhere to walk.

It was cold. It was nineteen degrees and dropping.

Ensign had a couple bottles of water, but he had no food.

A dead battery was not something Ensign could remedy.

As the night went on, nobody stopped to help.

The next morning, it was the cold which woke Ensign from sleep. His legs were numb and sore from the winter freeze. The Sun was bright when Ensign took the shade from his windshield. He could hear cars zipping past him. Ensign reached for his phone...and he realized he had another problem to add to the list.

At first, he thought his phone was off. Then, he thought his phone had died. Finally, Ensign figured his phone was too cold, and it would turn on once it was warmed up. Ensign was wrong. His phone, at the worst possible time, had completely broken. Ensign still had a backup phone, the phone which held a charge for a maximum of ten minutes. He found the phone and plugged it into a battery pack.

The stress was overwhelming. Ensign made a conscious choice to spend the entire day hanging out and working on his car as if he were spending his leisure time there by choice. The stress of the trip, to that point, was enough to cause a reset in Ensign's brain. There on the side of the road, in that situation, Ensign took a mental vacation from everything. He was stranded, and his mind had checked out. Ensign did drugs and worked on various projects for the remainder of the day.

By nightfall, Ensign's focus shifted to his attempt to remain warm for one more night. After wrapping his legs in blankets, Ensign managed to get some sleep. The pain in Ensign's legs from the fifteen-degree night woke him up the next morning; the same as it had the day before. It was lightly snowing as Ensign stepped from his car to walk around and get some circulation in his legs. He almost fell over when he first tried to stand up outside the car. Ensign's legs were in bad shape. He managed to get the blood flowing after five minutes of walking around on the shoulder of the highway.

Ensign knew he had to do something that day. He had managed fine without food, but he was down to half a bottle of semi-frozen water. Ensign emptied out his backpack. He grabbed a socket wrench and popped the hood of his car. After removing the battery, Ensign put the wrench away. He scribbled a note on a piece of paper and left it on the dashboard of his car, visible from outside the front windshield. Ensign didn't want his car to be towed in his absence.

"Stranded. Walked to find phone service. Back shortly."

With the extremely heavy car battery in his backpack and the receipt for it in his pocket, Ensign grabbed his backup phone and began walking up the hill of the overpass. Once he reached the point where the overpass dropped off to the road below, he climbed over the guardrail and worked his way down the steep slope to the surface street. Ensign, exhausted from hiking with the battery on his back, walked along the side of the road below the interstate overpass.

Ensign powered on his backup phone. He sat down on the car battery to rest and catch his breath. Ensign knew, once his phone booted up, that he would only have an extremely limited timeframe to find phone service and contact a ride service. Ensign checked the bars on his phone; nothing. He held the phone up above his head. A single bar appeared. It wasn't enough reception to use the ride service app, but it gave him hope. Ensign left his backpack and battery where he had been sitting, and he walked down the road. Eventually, Ensign's backup phone showed three bars of service.

"Your ride is fifteen minutes away."

"Your ride has been cancelled."

"Your ride is seventeen minutes away."

"Your ride has been cancelled…"

After time passed, Ensign's phone was dangerously low on power. He managed to reach a driver on the app. Just before Ensign's phone died, he sent the driver one final message.

"This location is where I am for sure. Please show up. My phone will die in the next minute or so. I will be here. Please help me. I'll see you in twenty minutes."

Twenty minutes passed. Ensign was about to give up hope when he saw a car approaching from the curve up ahead. He waved his hands. The car pulled up and stopped. It was his driver. Ensign promised the driver a huge tip for taking the time to help him. The driver had been planning to go off duty and go home for the day. Had it not been for that one driver, Ensign wouldn't have had any other options. Ensign charged his phone in the car. Forty-five minutes later, Ensign was dropped off at his Subaru with a new battery. Ensign made sure to tip the driver the maximum amount before his phone died again.

That night, after more than two weeks, Ensign finally left Kentucky. He made it out. His car had no more issues on his drive south. After a couple more days, and a couple of nights of sleep at rest stops along the way, Ensign reached Florida. It was past the middle of February in 2021. The weather was warm and sunny. The trip was behind him. Ensign made it.

Torpor

Having almost frozen to death earlier in the week, the Florida heat was a pleasant change. When Ensign reached the Tampa Bay area, he decided the first thing he needed was a new phone. Ensign's phone bill was overdue. Ensign decided to buy a new phone and switch his number over to the new phone when he paid the bill. That didn't work out. The phone company wasn't able to switch the number, so Ensign didn't pay the bill. Instead, for the first time in thirteen years, Ensign got a new phone number. That turned out to be a big mistake. Ensign's email accounts were attached to his old phone number. Ensign lost everything attached to his old phone number. He was locked out. Without that number, Ensign had to create a new primary email.

After sending Shannon a message to let her know he was finally in her area, Ensign got on the website and began reaching out to people in Tampa. Fortunately, the website was still accessible on Ensign's new phone. As Ensign sat in the parking lot of the electronics store, messages began coming in on the website. Shannon replied to Ensign's text message. She was amazed that he actually made it to Florida. They made plans to see each other the following day. Ensign then went back to finding someone to stay with that night. He reached out and got a response.

"Meet me at the front gates at eleven o'clock. I'll buzz you in."

"I'll be able to find you at the front gates?"

"You will. I'll be driving my golf cart."

The trans woman Ensign planned to meet was a couple of years older than him. She had been in contact with Ensign the last time he was in Florida, but their schedules hadn't lined up. When Ensign told her he was back in the area, she invited him to stay with her at her house. Ensign was relieved. He was looking forward to showering, and he was fairly sure he was going to be sleeping in an actual bed that night.

"I'm done. I can't do anymore. That's the most I've ever done at one time. I've never even seen that much at one time."

"No worries. I'll finish it up myself."

Ensign blew down the last two large lines of crystal from his silver tray and packed his equipment back into his bag. He walked back into the bedroom and put his bag next to his backpack on the side of the bed. Ensign grabbed his clothes and shoes, and he walked back out into the living room. Ensign dressed as he asked what the plan was for the rest of the night. Leslie responded while she was also in the process of putting her clothes back on.

"I need to get another six pack. I'm out of beer."

"Alright. I only have one seat in my camper/car…"

"We're taking my golf cart. The carry-out is right up the street."

"Are you good to drive it? How much have you had to drink?"

"I'm good. I haven't had enough. That's why I need to get more."

"I can drive it, since I don't drink…"

"I got it. I go there every day. It's just a quarter mile up the road once we get to the other side of this community. I'm good. I promise."

Five minutes and a bunch of speedbumps later, Leslie and Ensign reached the far side of Leslie's neighborhood. Leslie pulled the golf cart out onto the road alongside the community of manufactured homes where she lived. Ensign could see the gas station up in front of them on the right side of the road. Ensign looked behind him. He saw headlights approaching behind the golf cart.

"There's a car coming behind us."

"I see it. It's fine."

Leslie and Ensign reached the gas station as the car behind the golf cart reached Leslie and Ensign. As Leslie turned the wheel to pull into the parking lot, Ensign looked back in time to watch the police car pull into the gas station behind them. Leslie muttered something under her breath. Ensign looked over at her.

"What?"

"Every day…these guys mess with me every day."

"Uh…I hope that doesn't mean something's about to happen."

Leslie jumped from the golf cart and hurried towards the store entrance. An officer stepped from his cruiser. He spoke.

"Come over here a second."

Leslie held out a finger to signal him to wait, and she walked into the gas station. Surprisingly, the officer waited outside. A second officer stepped from the passenger side of the car. Ensign remained seated in the golf cart. He waved a hand of acknowledgement to the police. Each officer nodded back in response.

Leslie came back outside five minutes later, a six-pack of beer in her left hand. One of the officers waved to get her attention. Ensign felt apprehension as he saw the scowl on Leslie's face. He tried to catch Leslie's eye before she could address the officers.

Leslie glanced at Ensign. He gave her a look to imply she needed to tread lightly with her interaction. Ensign knew Leslie had already been drinking. She was also driving a golf cart on public roads. Leslie turned back to face the officers.

"What?"

"We told ya the other day. Ya need a license plate if you're driving that golf cart outside yer community."

"Ok! I told you I'm working on it."

Leslie put the beer behind her as she sat down next to Ensign in the golf cart.

"We're not gonna tell ya again. If we see ya out here again without a plate, we're gonna ticket ya and impound the cart."

"Ok! Fine."

Ensign's eyes were wide as Leslie pulled the golf cart out of the parking space and drove back to the road. He watched the officers as they walked into the gas station. Leslie pulled back onto the road and headed back towards her house. Ensign breathed a sigh of relief. Leslie swore under her breath the rest of the way back home. Ensign was fairly certain Leslie wasn't in condition to drive a golf cart that evening, despite Leslie's previous assurance otherwise.

Self-Sabotage

Florida; the Sunshine State. It was bright and sunny the next morning when Ensign left Leslie's house. He had things to do; a car to work on, laundry to wash, food to eat, drugs to consume. Ensign drove through the Tampa Bay area. He reached out to Shannon. They picked a time to meet up at a gas station. Ensign found a park close to the particular gas station. It was on the water. It was a good place for him to get some more work done on his car.

A couple of hours later, Ensign packed up his tools. He was pouring sweat. The Florida heat was in full effect. Ensign drove five minutes down the road to the gas station. Ten minutes later, Shannon pulled into a parking space next to Ensign's Subaru. Ensign gladly stepped from his car to hers. Ensign's air conditioning in the Subaru camper/car didn't work. The air conditioning in Shannon's car was on, full blast, as the two of them got high and engaged in car intimacy.

After Shannon went on her way, Ensign remained in the parking lot. He painted his car. He worked on the stereo system as the night sky grew dark. There was a twenty-four-hour laundromat in the strip mall on the far side of the parking lot. Ensign began to do laundry in the middle of the night.

Ensign heard something behind him as he sat on the sidewalk outside of the laundromat at three o'clock in the morning. He looked back. He was surprised to see a raccoon running towards him on its hind legs. Ensign jumped to his feet to face the raccoon. He yelled at it.

"Get out of here! I'll kick you in the dick!"

The raccoon, startled by Ensign's voice, switched its trajectory. It remained on its hind legs but took off to the left and around the corner of the building. Ensign stayed on alert from that moment until his laundry finished as dawn broke the next morning. As time passed, no other wildlife tested him.

Ensign loaded up his car with clean clothes as the then-bustling parking lot filled with an absurd number of early morning work commuters. Ensign put his car in gear and joined the fray. The Sun was up when Ensign crossed over the Sunshine Skyway Bridge to reach the south side of the metro Tampa area. He found a rest stop on the side of the highway. That was where he posted up to do more work on his car.

Ensign had been in contact with a trans girl from an app on his phone since the last time he was in Florida. Chloe lived in Orlando. Ensign was a few hours away, but he agreed to visit Chloe when she invited him over to her house that day. Ensign packed up his tools once more, and he put Chloe's address into his phone's GPS. He sent an ETA in a text message, and he pulled out from the rest stop.

Later that night, Ensign pulled into the gas station parking lot back where he met Shannon the day before. He was tired from driving to Orlando to see Chloe and then returning to Tampa later that same evening. Ensign had been looking forward to the soft-serve ice cream at that particular Tampa gas station since he left Orlando earlier that day. Ensign turned off his car after he pulled into a parking space at the gas station.

Instantly, Ensign lost his car keys. He hadn't even gotten up from the driver's seat of his car. He literally turned off his car, pulled the keys from the ignition, and suddenly his keys were gone. Crystal meth accounted for Ensign's actions for the next hour and a half. He moved around, he looked all over, multiple times he unloaded and reloaded all the items packed in his camper/car. Ensign wanted ice cream, but he was stuck in his car looking for his keys.

After an hour and a half, Ensign's tweaked brain finally felt relief. He managed to find his keys. They had fallen into the crack between the driver's seat and the backrest to the seat. At eleven thirty that night, Ensign finally locked up his car and walked inside to get ice cream from the gas station. He was pouring sweat from the crystal-fueled frantic key searching over the previous hour and a half. Absorbed in drug-induced paranoia, Ensign thought everyone in the gas station knew he spent all that time looking for his keys.

During the next few weeks, Ensign stayed busy. He tattooed himself at the beach below the bridge over Tampa Bay. He met up with Shannon and did car stuff with her on a regular basis. Ensign continued to work on his car at different rest stops and parks in the Tampa area. Ensign met random people from the website and on the apps. He also met random people he came across while he lived the car life in Florida.

Ensign got a call from Shannon one morning. She had a new job, and her new company put her up in a hotel in Jacksonville so she could attend meetings and conferences. Shannon invited Ensign to join her across the state in Jacksonville for those three days. Ensign accepted the invitation. He agreed to meet Shannon at the hotel when she checked in.

Ensign's car drove without issue across the state to Jacksonville. Ensign and Shannon recorded videos together in the hotel room. They did drugs together. While Shannon attended meetings, Ensign remained at the hotel. He did drugs and created requested videos which he sent to Shannon. One particular evening, Shannon wanted to dye Ensign's hair. They went to the store and picked up hair dye. Shannon then dyed Ensign's hair in the hotel room.

When the time came to check out, Shannon went her separate way back to the Tampa area on the west side of Florida. Ensign took a detour. He headed south from Jacksonville to visit Liam again in Titusville. Ensign hadn't seen Liam since he previously stayed with him in Titusville after leaving his living situation with Zoe back in 2019.

Ensign's car began to drive funny on the trip to see Liam. During his time at Liam's house that next week, Ensign attempted to diagnose and fix the Subaru. Liam and Ensign did drugs around the clock. Liam's demeanor shifted from welcoming to paranoid. Liam was convinced that Ensign's presence in the retirement community would lead to neighbors reporting him for violating community guidelines. Ensign, not wishing to add stress to Liam's life, left to head back to Tampa at eleven o'clock at night. It was a week after Ensign arrived from Jacksonville. Ensign's welcome had run its course.

Ensign, five minutes after leaving Liam's house, was pulled over by the police before he could even clear Titusville. It was dark outside at eleven o'clock that night. The wiring in Ensign's Subaru was causing issues. He had no rear lights as he drove. Ensign convinced the officer to allow him to drive back to Liam's for the night and then make the drive to Tampa the next morning in the daylight.

Liam wasn't happy when Ensign showed up again shortly after leaving his house. Liam thought he was safe from neighbor complaints without any visitors. Liam once again had a visitor. He let Ensign back inside, but he immediately went to bed. Liam had to work early the next morning. Ensign stayed up and blew down hotrail after hotrail to try to improve his evening.

The next morning, Liam and Ensign hugged. Liam apologized for his lack of hospitality, and he explained to Ensign how he feared being kicked out of the community. Ensign thanked Liam for the one more night of having him there. When Liam went to work, Ensign drove back across the state to Tampa.

Ensign watched sunrises and sunsets over the water from the beach on the Sunshine Skyway Bridge. He tattooed himself as he sat outside his car in the sand. Cars were allowed to drive on the sand of that particular beach. Ensign watched kite-boarders in the water. He was included in other people's cookouts on the beach. He ate hamburgers, hot dogs, and potato salad. He took soap with him into the bay to wash up amongst the saltwater waves.

When Ensign left the beach, he worked on the air intake and hoses under the hood of the Subaru at various parking lots around the Tampa area. He met up with Shannon periodically. Ensign tried out new restaurants in the area. He continued to interact with people on his phone. He continued to do drugs constantly. Ensign still had a good amount of crystal with him. His money was running low. He made a one-time deal with someone he knew. He sold the last eightball he could spare. The rest of his drugs were strictly his personal supply.

Ensign took a drive down the west coast of the state to Fort Meyers. A lady from the website was housesitting at one of her friend's houses for a week. She invited Ensign to spend time with her at the house. Ensign's car made the multi-hour drive. Ensign navigated the surface streets of Fort Meyers. He was not impressed with the city as he drove through it. He eventually reached the house. Cher greeted Ensign with a hug and kiss at the front door.

Ensign's first night at the house in Fort Meyers did not include sleep. Cher went to bed. Ensign didn't. Cher didn't do crystal, and she wasn't thrilled to find out that Ensign was always zooted on the stuff. Ensign was paranoid all night. At one point, Ensign opened a drawer in the kitchen to grab a fork. He instantly yelled and jumped back in reaction to a drawer completely full of cockroaches of all sizes.

The next night, Cher went to sleep again. Ensign remained awake yet another night. At that point, Ensign passed beyond the audio-hallucination period to full on hallucinating. In the dark of night, Ensign peeked out of the blinds to the patio in the backyard. Ensign saw four people outside of the sliding glass back door. He took cover behind the couch and pulled out his gun. Ensign aimed and held steady for the next hour. Nothing happened, so Ensign cautiously crept his way to the door. With his handgun aimed to the backyard, he quickly pulled the curtain back. Nobody was there. Later that night, the scenario repeated. Again, Ensign pulled the curtain back and pointed his gun. Again, nobody was there.

Cher went to work the next day. Ensign stayed at the house. He did drugs, he interacted on his phone, he worked out, and he managed a short nap. When he woke up, the hallucinations were gone. Cher arrived back at the house after her workday ended. Cher and Ensign had a talk. Cher had ended a previous relationship due to meth consumption. Cher and Ensign decided that Ensign wasn't what Cher needed in her life at that point. Ensign left Fort Meyers. Again, he headed back to the Tampa area.

It was evening as Ensign drove across the multiple-mile bridge over Tampa Bay. Ensign was hot and sweaty. He was exhausted. He was in a bad mood. Ensign was halfway across the bridge, out in the middle of the bay. Ensign's Subaru ran out of gas.

"I'm over it. I don't care anymore."

"Ensign, where are you?"

"I'll send you a text with the mile marker and road. After that, I'm going to sleep."

Ensign hung up the phone. He found a mile marker close to where his car had stopped. The expanse of roadway across Tampa Bay was a series of bridges and small islands of land supporting the pavement of the road. Ensign's car had come to a stop almost halfway across the bay, on one of the small islands in the middle of the water. There was enough room for his car to sit between the pavement and the guardrail where the water of the bay began. Ensign was facing north, over two miles from reaching the top of the bay. There were two miles of water behind him on the south side of the bay. Ensign was in the middle of Tampa Bay.

Ensign texted his location to his lifelong friend, Andrea. He needed to sleep, and he turned off his phone. Ensign had hardly slept during the previous week, so he knew he was about to crash hard. The heat was going to be a concern. He had to keep his windows up; mosquitos were a far more immediate issue that night.

Ensign woke up the next morning as he cooked in the Sun. He sat up, soaked in sweat. He saw a tow truck parked behind him. The driver was walking towards Ensign's Subaru with a can of gasoline. As the tow truck driver emptied the contents into Ensign's gas tank, he explained the situation to Ensign.

"I work for AAA. We got a call that someone was stranded out here. The police have already been out here."

"Huh?" Ensign was still in the process of waking up.

"They knocked on the windows, but you didn't wake up. Your friend called us again to check on you."

"What's that?"

"I only have one gallon of gas for you, but it will get you off of this bridge."

Ensign was confused. He assumed it was Andrea who helped him out, but he didn't understand the part about the police. How did the tow truck driver know the police had been out earlier in the morning? Why would they have just left when they got no response as they tried to wake him? Whatever. Once the tow truck driver drove away, Ensign blew down a hotrail.

Ensign drove across the rest of the bridge and then to the first gas station he saw. He fueled up. He got ice cream. He changed out of his clothes, clothes which were completely soaked in sweat. Ensign wrung out the shirt he had been wearing overnight. Ensign's sweat dripped down to the pavement in the gas station parking lot as he stood outside his car in the hot Florida sunlight.

Ensign didn't know it, but he had been on a timer; one which was about to expire. It was a timer which began all the way back in 2018, when Ensign first began his new life of travel and exploration; back when he made that deal with himself. Through all that had happened over those years, Ensign's trajectory still seemed to be upward in 2021. That timer...it was set to expire at the apex of the upward climb. The good on that journey upward somehow always outweighed the bad. Ensign's mental state had precariously endured. His travels and experiences somehow had a net positive through those years of adventure. Ensign had been through so much and still pressed onward with his unique form of wishful optimism, an optimism always juxtaposed against his doom and gloom depression. It was all fun and games...until suddenly it wasn't...

Proprioception

There was a nice suburb city just outside Tampa where Shannon lived. Ensign saw many similarities between Westchase and his home city of Perrysburg. The two cities were close in population and demographics. Ensign spent time with Shannon in Westchase when she was available to see him. Ensign spent the rest of his time exploring the Tampa area and working on his camper/car.

Ensign still had a good reserve of crystal for personal use. Shannon got high with him when they spent time together. Ensign would do a hotrail and blow the smoke into Shannon's mouth as they kissed. Though Ensign knew he was good for a while on his supply of drugs, he had another worry building. Each day, little by little, Ensign's money was running out.

Per usual, Ensign pulled into a small parking lot alongside a neighborhood in Westchase when Shannon told him she was done working for the day. Ensign turned off his car and waited. Ten minutes later, Shannon pulled up alongside Ensign's Subaru in the parking lot. Ensign grabbed his bag of drug supplies and a bag of adult novelty items, and he hopped into the passenger seat of Shannon's SUV.

Per usual, Shannon and Ensign slowly rolled around the neighborhood until they found a good place to park; one which was away from any public traffic. Shannon had dark tinted windows in her car, but the two of them still tried to remain as inconspicuous as possible when they engaged in illicit activity. Once Shannon parked, Ensign pulled out his bag of drug supplies and got to work lining up hotrails on his tray.

Ensign blew down three large lines of crystal. Each time he

did a hotrail, he kissed the smoke to Shannon. Ensign had been using crystal all day, but Shannon hadn't. Ensign could see the drugs take hold of Shannon as the two of them sat in the car on the street in the quiet neighborhood. Ensign then opened his other bag. Right there in Shannon's car, the two of them acted out whatever fantasies Shannon wished to do. Ensign was at peak arousal obeying Shannon's wishes. He loved the dynamic between them.

A brief time later, Shannon dropped Ensign off at his Subaru. As Shannon pulled away, Ensign decided he wanted to drive back to the rest stop on the Sunshine Skyway Bridge. He had spent many nights at that rest stop since he arrived in Florida. Ensign put his key in the ignition of the Subaru and turned it...and nothing happened. He tried again; still nothing. Ensign checked under the hood. He adjusted some things. He checked some items inside the car. He turned the key again...nothing.

Half an hour later, Ensign received bad news from Shannon. Shannon's new company had fired her after receiving a bill from the hotel she shared with Ensign in Jacksonville. The bill was a damage and cleaning fee for the hotel room. According to the hotel, eight hundred dollars in damages were accrued; including fees for hair dye in the bathroom and on the towels, as well as ruined sheets and bedding. The company fired Shannon over the phone half an hour after Ensign realized he was no longer mobile in his camper/car. Ensign was stranded in a broken car and suddenly not on good terms with Shannon at the same time.

That evening, right there in that small parking lot next to a neighborhood in Westchase, Florida...that was the exact point Ensign's multi-year trajectory reached its pinnacle. That moment, on that warm evening in spring of 2021; that was the exact moment when Ensign's life changed direction completely and permanently.

Ensign sat in his car and stared straight ahead. He knew his life had flipped upside-down. He also knew he wasn't prepared for anything from that moment on. Without a working vehicle, all of Ensign's website connections were no longer in reach. Without transportation, Ensign's homelessness was suddenly confined to his immediate location.

Fear crept into Ensign's mind. Ensign reclined his driver's seat. It moved back two inches. All his belongings were packed into the camper/car all around him. Ensign sprayed himself with bug spray...and he went to sleep. Prior to slumbering, his last thought was comforting; one day he would go to sleep and not have to wake up.

Heat, as usual, was what woke Ensign up the next morning. He found his bearings as he remembered that his car no longer worked. Ensign took a deep breath and reached for his drug bag. A couple of hotrails later, Ensign decided he needed to do something to fix his situation. His car had no cover from the Sun. It was morning, and the Sun was already cooking the Subaru.

There was a small pond and some trees adjacent to where Ensign was parked. As Ensign relieved himself amongst the trees, he decided which direction he was going to push his car. Ensign could see into the neighborhood. He decided to push his car down the street until he found a location with an overhanging tree to provide shade during the warmest portion of the day.

Within an hour, Ensign was sitting in his car again. Sweat was pouring off of him. He was exhausted, but he was in some shade deep into the neighborhood in Westchase. Ensign was parked on the street beneath an overhanging tree. He was surrounded by houses and sidewalks in a normal neighborhood in suburbia. His broken-down, crazy painted, out of state camper/car; a car packed full of all his belongings, stuck out in the normalcy of the neighborhood. The fact that the camper/car was where Ensign currently resided was even more conspicuous.

Ensign knew he was in for a rough time. Life was complicated....and the urgency of the situation was overwhelming. His repeated car hardships continued to accumulate and wear on his psyche. Consistent and excessive drug use, lack of proper sleep, and legitimately being homeless had Ensign slipping further off the edge than ever.

Ensign did some more hotrails of crystal methamphetamine as he took it all in. Moments later, he stepped from his super-heated car into the sunlight of the hot Florida afternoon. Moments after that, Ensign received his first dirty looks from the first of the neighbors who were out walking in the neighborhood.

A Quiet and Unassuming Life in Ordinary Circumstances

The flowers alongside the walkway in Hassan's front yard were in full bloom. The smell was delightful. Hassan smiled as he stepped outside and basked in the sunlight of the spring afternoon. Mrs. Johnson waved to him as she walked her dog on the sidewalk across the street. Hassan returned her wave, nodding his head towards his neighbor. Birds chirped randomly from the trees. The sky, deep and blue, was free of clouds. Hassan saw neighborhood children riding their bikes in the street a few houses down.

Hassan took a deep breath and stretched his arms above his head. Since Hassan worked from home, he made it a point to step outside for a few minutes every couple of hours for a break and some fresh air. As Hassan stood there on his small cement front porch, he focused on the sight; familiar over the prior two days. His smile slipped, just slightly. As he began to walk into the lawn of his front yard, Hassan asked the same question he had already asked earlier that day.

"Nothing yet?"

The answer came back to him as it had before.

"No. Not yet."

Hassan stood there on his lawn between his house and the street. He scrunched his face into an expression of concern. Hassan turned to walk back inside. He let go of one more sentence as he stepped into his house and shut the front door.

"Let me know if you need anything."

Ensign watched the front door shut. He felt bad, almost a sense of shame, as he picked up his socket wrench and got back to work on his car. Since Hassan first introduced himself to Ensign, he had provided Ensign with food and drinks. He took Ensign to the auto parts store twice to pick up parts which Ensign thought would fix his car. Hassan offered to pay for the parts, but Ensign covered the costs himself. Hassan had even offered to start a neighborhood fund to send Ensign back North and have his car shipped to meet him there. Ensign couldn't grasp the thought of traveling across the country separately from all of his most important and valuable belongings; an entire camper/car full of his life.

Ensign felt anxiety from the hospitality. He felt the only way he could pay back the favors was to get his car running again, and out of the street in front of Hassan's house. To that point, Ensign's attempts to make good were miserably failing. Though Ensign appreciated the hospitality, he knew he was quickly wearing out his welcome.

Ensign experienced a multitude of reactions while stranded in Westchase. Hassan had been on the far positive end of the spectrum of reactions to Ensign's sudden arrival in the quiet Florida neighborhood. Stress was building up in Ensign's compromised brain. Each new stressor added to Ensign's urgency as he was hit from every angle around him.

In the beginning, the dirty looks were balanced out with waves and greetings from random passers-by. Soon, Ensign noticed odd behavior. It made him uncomfortable. Cars drove past him in his Subaru. As they approached, they slowed down. Ensign saw the occupants of the cars recording videos as they passed. Sometimes Ensign saw neighbors recording videos as they stood outside down the street. Paranoia skyrocketed. Why was he suddenly the focus of videos being recorded by people in the neighborhood? The answer came to Ensign by way of an unusual messenger.

Ensign had just put away his pipe and stepped from his car one afternoon when a man on a bike suddenly skidded to a stop at the front of Ensign's car. Ensign, startled by the bike rider, flinched as the man hopped off the bike.

"You're famous around here right now. Two thousand views on the neighborhood group chat in the past two hours. What's your name? I'm Scott."

"Wha…what are you talking about?"

"Sit down and eat lunch with me. My name's Scott. What's your name?"

As Scott sat down on the curb, he handed Ensign a happy meal from McDonald's. Scott had another happy meal for himself. Scott opened his happy meal and began to eat. Ensign cautiously took the food he was offered.

"What, you aren't hungry? Sit. Eat. Your name's Ensign, right? Let's get to know each other."

Ensign slowly sat down next to Scott. He thanked Scott for the food. As Ensign removed a cheeseburger from the colorful box, he cautiously confirmed his name to Scott. He then followed with two questions for Scott.

"What are you talking about; I'm 'famous?' How'd you know my name?"

"You're a big deal this week. Here, look. You're the biggest news in the area."

Ensign's heart sank as he looked at the phone Scott held in front of him. There it was all up in his face: post after post on the neighborhood's social media page, different views and angles of Ensign and his broken-down camper/car. Pictures and videos, all with hundreds (a couple with thousands) of comments and views. Ensign felt awful. All he wanted was to fix his car and be on his way. He wanted as little attention as possible. He was suddenly and embarrassingly trending as a circus novelty.

As Ensign slowly chewed his food, he read comments on the posts Scott showed him. Some commenters were sympathetic and compassionate. Some were angry and downright awful with their words. Ensign wanted nothing but to disappear as he sat there on the curb in the Florida sunlight. Ensign's nightmare paranoia became real life as his tweaked brain tried to process the sudden exposure to so many people at one of the lowest points in his life. It was beyond embarrassing. Ensign was at a loss. Scott saw the mortification on Ensign's face, and he quickly tried to find words to put Ensign at ease.

"It's ok buddy. We just want to know what's going on, and we want to help you. Don't pay attention to those negative commenters. They don't know anything."

"Uh…"

"Hassan first posted to the neighborhood group. You told him your story, didn't you? He wanted to see if we could help you out. All us neighbors just want to see you get going again."

Ensign was still frozen without words. Suddenly, he was overflowing with speech at a panicked rate. Words began to spill out in incomplete thoughts and sentences.

"I need to get out of…I need to explain myself…I don't want… I just want to fix my car…"

"It's ok buddy. Add me as friend. Stay in touch. You'll be alright." Scott handed Ensign the toy from his happy meal. "Here, take mine."

Ensign managed a smile. Scott hopped back on his bike and rode away, waving as he told Ensign he would see him again soon. Ensign looked at the happy meal toy in his hand, and he felt his eyes water up. He just wanted to leave, and he couldn't. He was stuck right there in the middle of a public humiliation, fully exposed at a low point in life…and some of those people were far from sympathetic.

Scott and Ensign became friends on the social media platform, and Scott accepted Ensign's request to join the neighborhood group on the site. Ensign posted on the group's home page. He introduced himself. He explained his travel and how he had broken down. He apologized for being a burden to anyone wishing he were gone. He explained he meant no ill will…he just wanted to get his car running again so he could be on his way. Ensign soon erased his post and exited the group. He just wished he could disappear. He didn't want the attention at all.

As days went by, people continued to drive by and record video. Some people came by with food and cases of bottled water. Sometimes people even asked for an order from local restaurants and came back from the restaurants to eat with him at his car. A local news reporter attempted to interview him. She then gave Ensign a hundred dollars and picked him up three sub sandwiches from a local sub shop. Ensign was grateful for the help, but it was thoroughly embarrassing.

The dirty looks continued as well. So did visits from police. At one point, two officers bought Ensign lunch and ate with him as they questioned him about his plans to get running again. Ensign was lost. He had no idea what he was going to do. It was an early morning visit from a police officer on day ten when Ensign reached his breaking point. Though the officer was cordial, the message was clear that multiple residents of the neighborhood wanted Ensign gone immediately. When the officer drove away, Ensign went into autopilot. He didn't think, he just acted. He couldn't remain in that situation a single minute longer.

The Nash Equilibrium

There were no clouds in the sky. It was bright outside. It was hot. Ensign's car was all the way in the back of the Westchase neighborhood. Ensign hopped into the driver's seat and put the key in the ignition. He switched gears to neutral, and he stepped back out onto the street. With one hand on the steering wheel and the other on the frame of the door, Ensign began to push.

He pushed as he guided the steering wheel. He pushed his car all the way to the other end of the street. Ensign took a break at the turn. He wiped sweat from his face, and he chugged down a bottle of water. Then he pushed some more.

Ensign navigated turns and stopped at stop signs. He ignored the random people who chose to record video instead of helping him. He pushed out and around a car which pulled up in front of him to keep him from stopping on a particular length of road. As Ensign pushed his car by himself in the heat, the occupants of the car watched from their air-conditioned seats in their running vehicle. It took extra pushing and steering at the same time to maneuver his way around the car. An hour passed. Ensign kept going. After three other streets of pushing, Ensign and his car reached the far-side entrance to the neighborhood.

The road outside the neighborhood was congested with traffic. It was two lanes in each direction, and the speed limit was forty-five miles an hour. Ensign barely bothered to not get hit as he pushed his car out of the neighborhood and into the traffic. He kept pushing his car in the right travel lane. Cars slowed down and moved over into the other lane to avoid hitting him. Ensign's mind was elsewhere. Nobody stopped to help. Ensign continued by himself in the heat for a full eight-tenths of a mile to the first stoplight intersection down the street.

It was then, at the red light of that intersection, that a lady in a car behind him offered her help. Ensign hopped into his Subaru. When the light turned green, the lady pushed Ensign's car with her car through the intersection. Ensign, barely able to speak from the heat and the activity, thanked the lady as he began pushing his car again. There was an entrance to a Costco parking lot another quarter mile ahead of him on the right. Ensign didn't make it that far.

Completely exhausted, Ensign only made it to the beginning of the turn lane for the Costco. His body gave out from the heat and exertion. Ensign grabbed a folding chair from the back of his Subaru and managed to walk it over to the grass on the side of the road. He left his car there in the turn lane as he sat in the chair and battled against unconsciousness. Ensign gave up. He didn't have any energy left to push his car the rest of the way. Ensign closed his eyes as he sat in the folding chair in the grass of that field. The sunlight faded to black. The sounds of the traffic on the busy roads, and in the intersection behind him, faded away to silence.

The sound startled Ensign awake. Ensign was lost in a fog of reanimation. The air around him was warm and bright. Ensign was seated in a chair. There was grass under his feet. A shopping complex came into focus in the distance. The noise around him was from traffic. Ensign heard the sound again. That time, he knew what it was. It came from behind him. Ensign stood up and turned around. The source of the sound, as expected, was there in the road behind his broken-down vehicle.

Two police cruisers, with lights flashing, were parked on the street. The officer, the one who used the siren to wake Ensign, stepped from his cruiser to join the other two officers as they talked in the road. Ensign folded up his chair and walked to meet the police as they stood between their cars and the Subaru camper/car. Ensign readied himself to explain his situation again and attempt to garner sympathy and help.

Moments later, from the driver's seat, Ensign guided his car into a parking space at the fast-food restaurant on the corner of the intersection. The police had pushed as Ensign steered the rest of the way in the turn lane, onto the auxiliary road to Costco, and into the parking lot of the restaurant. Ensign thanked the officers for their assistance. Before the police left the scene, one officer pulled out a digital camera and took multiple pictures of Ensign's camper/car.

In the moment, Ensign didn't care. He was simply happy to be done pushing his car for the time being. Life was difficult, exhausting, and immediate. Ensign blew down a hotrail of crystal as he sat in his car and rested. He was fully spent. The drugs barely had any effect on him physically, but they helped put his mind at ease. Ensign had no idea what step to take next in his life. Suddenly, the idea came to him. He was going to walk into the restaurant and buy some chicken strips, chicken strips with ketchup and buffalo sauce.

In the middle of the night, four nights later, Ensign again sprayed himself with bug spray. The mosquitos were relentless. Though nobody at the fast-food restaurant said anything to Ensign about being parked in their parking lot, the crystal made him as paranoid as ever. Ensign felt exposed. The fast-food restaurant was situated on the corner of the intersection. Anyone who drove by, on either of the roads, had a clear view into the parking lot; empty except for the very noticeable camper/car. One more hotrail, and Ensign decided he needed to make a change.

In Ensign's mind, he planned his route. He was going to push his car across the parking lot, taking a right onto the auxiliary road between the restaurant and the much larger Costco parking lot. Once on the auxiliary road, Ensign would need to take a left about twenty feet farther, and then he could cross the open pavement to reach the parking spaces at the very back of the Costco lot.

Ensign knew the task was about to be extremely challenging.

There were three storm drains in the fast-food restaurant's parking lot. The pavement angled down sharply where it led to each drain. Ensign would need enough momentum as he headed toward each dip in the parking lot to then be able to get his car up the opposite side of pavement beyond each storm drain. Ensign would have to steer his car while he pushed it across the lot. Once to the other side, he would need to push the car up the pavement which led to the auxiliary road. While guiding the steering wheel, Ensign would then need to make it over another incline as he turned into the Costco lot.

Ensign set up his phone in the holder hanging down from the center of his windshield. He recorded four hours of attempts to make it across the three storm drains in the restaurant parking lot. Finally, after many attempts, he made it to the auxiliary road. Ensign was pouring sweat. On the verge of passing out, he took a break to do drugs while his car sat between the two parking lots. Half an hour later, Ensign's camper/car was lined up in a parking space at the back of the Costco lot. He made it… and he fell asleep almost instantly.

A noise above Ensign woke him up a couple short hours later. The first blues of sunrise began to lighten the sky from the black of night. Ensign looked up through his windshield. He saw the source of the noise. A news helicopter was hovering high above his parked car. Was Ensign hallucinating? Was the helicopter of the Tampa news anchor who previously gave Ensign a hundred dollars actually there in the sky above him?

Ensign recorded video as he stepped from his car in the early morning darkness. The video Ensign recorded proved to his chemically saturated brain that there had actually been a news helicopter in the sky above him for almost ten minutes. Ensign's tactic of recording videos set his mind at ease. It hadn't been the drugs. It had actually happened. Though his mind was eased by the video proof, his paranoia spiked due to a helicopter hovering above his car for almost ten minutes. Again, Ensign wished for nothing more than to disappear.

A Break in the Action

A shiny black Cadillac pulled into the parking space next to Ensign's Subaru. Ensign waved the smoke from in front of his face, and he stepped out of his car. A kindly older gentleman stepped from the Cadillac with something in his hand. The man handed Ensign a hundred-dollar bill. Ensign thanked the gentleman for his charity.

Three mornings later, Ensign heard another car pull up close to where he was parked. Ensign peeked through the crack of his window shade and instantly grabbed his drug paraphernalia, stashing it out of sight. He waved the smoke from in front of him as he quickly stepped from his car. Ensign walked to meet the police officer between his Subaru and the cruiser parked two spaces over. Ensign readied himself to tell his story once again.

Ensign's time, after his interaction with law enforcement, was then dedicated to pushing his car to another parking lot. The officer had explained that Ensign needed to be somewhere else besides Costco. Ensign had complied. Later that day, Ensign saw Shannon pull up next to him in the parking lot of the small grocery store adjacent to Costco. After he sat down next to Shannon in her car, Ensign explained his situation; what he had been through since he previously lost contact with her. Shannon called a tow truck for Ensign.

As summer began in Florida in 2021, Ensign spent three full weeks in a Walmart parking lot. He met the other people who lived in their cars in that same parking lot. He worked on his car. He continued to do drugs and interact with people online. Sometimes, Shannon came to visit him. They would share intimacy in her car after they did drugs. Shannon went shopping for non-perishable groceries with Ensign at the Walmart. Shannon and Ensign were the only two English-speaking people inside the Walmart; Ensign heard no other customers or employees speaking English on any of his visits. Everyone else spoke exclusively Spanish.

Ensign found two grams of crystal in his car one day while sorting through his belongings. He added it to his ever-dwindling supply of methamphetamine. Ensign walked around the strip mall complex when he couldn't stand sitting in his hot car any longer. He shopped at dollar stores, and he ate food from a food truck set up in the Walmart parking lot. Ensign did laundry at the laundromat down the street. Sometimes he pushed his car to different parking spaces. Ensign's chemically enhanced and sleep deprived mind was ever paranoid.

Ensign found an auto supply store, and he bought yet another new car battery. He then carried that battery down the street and all the way back across the Walmart parking lot; to the far side space where his car was parked. The battery worked. Ensign's car started. He couldn't drive it, though. The previous air intake hose arrangement, the one which Ensign rebuilt and created, caused the car to idle at maximum rpm anytime the car was turned on. Idling in park barely kept the Subaru from uncontrollably lurching forward.

There was a new character in Ensign's proximity. Samuel spoke English, so Ensign didn't have the language barrier as an excuse to avoid interaction. Samuel was a White gentleman in his late sixties. Samuel, same as Ensign, lived in his car in the Walmart parking lot in Tampa, Florida. According to Samuel, he had lived at that Walmart for a full three years when Ensign arrived. Ensign did what he could to keep exchanges with Samuel to a minimum. Patience with Samuel ran thin.

For the first time in days, Ensign managed to fall asleep. The much-needed rest was interrupted. Samuel continued to knock on the window of Ensign's car. The knocking continued, even after Ensign pulled down the shade to see who was outside the Subaru in the middle of the night. Ensign flung open the car door. Anger replaced exhaustion as Ensign engaged with Samuel. There was no avoiding that particular interaction. Samuel's sneak conversation attack as Ensign slept required immediate and appropriate countermeasures.

"What? What do you want, Sam?"

"Here, here's some peanut butter and some…"

"You seriously woke me up to give me half a used jar of peanut butter?"

"Yeah, I also have some…"

"I haven't slept all week. Get out of here. I don't want that."

"The tow truck is gonna come back on Tuesday…"

"Sam, get out of here!"

Samuel was right. The tow truck came back on Tuesday. The driver stopped at each long-term vehicle in the shopping center. Ensign was on edge already when the truck pulled up next to his Subaru. Ensign had questions. The driver of the tow truck had answers. From that conversation, stress increased. Paranoia skyrocketed when Ensign heard that the police were going to be cracking down on vehicles that long-term camped in the Walmart parking lot.

Hour by Hour

Ensign had shelter in his car. He had all of his most important items secure with him in his car. The time came. Ensign's paranoia won. In the course of one day, Ensign made a series of decisions; each markedly changed his life. Then, like that, Ensign didn't have anything anymore. Ensign lost everything in one day: his car, his belongings…Florida. They were gone.

Twenty-four hours of bad decisions resulted in bad situations; the situations led to more bad decisions…those decisions led to worse situations. In the time it took Earth to spin one rotation on its axis, the time between two o'clock in the morning on a Thursday and that same time on a Friday; in that brief time, everything went wrong. Decision after bad decision; those last twenty-four hours in Florida were nothing short of catastrophic.

2AM: Not again. Ensign knew immediately what woke him up. Samuel was still knocking on the glass when Ensign yanked the shade from his car window. Samuel looked startled, and he took a step back from the Subaru when he saw the look on Ensign's face.

"Never knock on my window again!"

"But the tow truck is coming for sure tomorrow."

"Sam! Never knock on my window again! If you don't see me outside my car, stay away from my car!"

Ensign angrily put the shade back up in the window of his car. Samuel walked back across the Walmart parking lot towards his own vehicle. Ensign's anger was soon replaced with exhaustion.

He had only been asleep for an hour when Samuel woke him up. Ensign again fell asleep in his Subaru as sweat covered his body. Sleep was a relief from the hot Florida night.

3AM: Ensign, deep in sleep, hadn't yet begun to dream. The hour passed; uneventful.

4AM: At peace, or as close to it as possible, Ensign half awoke to roll over onto his other side. He was never able to sleep too long in one position.

5AM: The dreams began. Short and intense, their theme was brought on by Samuel's warning. A particular dream had jolted Ensign awake just enough to be free of the particular nightmare. Once back asleep, a new nightmare took over Ensign's subconscious. Unrelenting; the nightmares pounded Ensign in his slumber.

6AM: Ensign quickly sat up and the dream disappeared from his mind. Instinctively, he started his car. The engine, at full RPM, shook the car quickly and violently. Ensign's body shook with the car and sweat dripped from his shaking body. Ensign hadn't had a single clear thought since he woke. He mashed his foot on the brake pedal and struggled to yank the car into gear.

Even using all his strength to stand and push on the brake pedal, Ensign couldn't hold his car from lurching forward once it was in gear. It took everything Ensign could muster to steer the Subaru and maintain a controlled speed at full throttle. It was as if he were riding a bull. All the power of a full-bore engine was barely held in control on a vehicle wanting nothing more than to open up at the fastest speed possible.

Ensign was fully physically drained in the few seconds it took him to frantically guide and govern his camper/car from its parking space to the dumpsters behind the shopping center. Ensign managed to turn the car off as he collapsed in his seat, out of breath and overheated. That couple-hundred-yard drive was the test. It took all of his strength to maintain control of his

Subaru at full throttle, but he managed it.

7AM: Ensign finished the purge of unnecessary items from his vehicle. Anything he absolutely didn't need, or anything he felt he couldn't sell at a pawn shop, Ensign tossed into the dumpsters behind the shopping center. His Subaru was half as packed as it had been before the trip to the dumpsters.

Ensign sat in the Subaru and mentally sorted two items. First, he planned his route. Once he began driving, he knew he wouldn't have any time to make corrections or amendments. Once he was sure of the path to take, Ensign began his next mental preparation. Ensign had to psych himself up. What he was about to do, by any standard, was absolutely insane. Ensign knew it, and he was scared.

There was no turning back once he committed to taking the action. Ensign began a countdown from ten. He stopped at seven. After some deep breaths, he let out a scream as he gripped the steering wheel. He began to count down again. Ensign stopped at four. He sat down in his driver's seat and caught his breath. He needed to mentally regroup. Ensign wasn't ready. The moment was overwhelming. Ensign shook as he prepared to begin the countdown again.

Ensign reached the bottom of ten. As the word "zero" escaped his lips, he turned the key in the ignition of the Subaru. His foot stomped on the brake pedal as the car jumped into drive. Ensign's mind exploded as the absolutely most hectic five minutes of his life began; right there next to those dumpsters, behind that shopping center, in Florida on a summer morning in 2021.

Ensign couldn't help but let out a scream as the Subaru ripped from park and tore down the pavement behind the shopping center. It was all he could do; to turn the wheel enough to stay out of the pond behind the crux at the backside of the shopping center. He managed to swerve around the right angle to continue down the other side, behind the buildings. A couple hundred yards ahead in the distance, the pavement opened up to the six-lane road adjacent to the shopping center. Ensign barely managed to turn the wheel enough to not jump the median once he rocketed out onto the public street. Ensign's car was smoking, and the noise was almost unbearable.

Everything shook as Ensign pushed his body from the roof of the car as he stomped, with all his might, continuously on the brake pedal to fight the open throttle. Ensign's camper/car screamed down the road, shaking violently as Ensign used all of his strength to barely control the vehicle. Ensign made it eight tenths of a mile down that road. He crossed six intersections of four-way traffic. Three of those intersections had traffic lights which were red; Ensign had no option but to run those red lights and dodge traffic the entire way. Ensign bombed across six lanes, and multiple curbs, to end up in the parking lot of the pawn shop which he had set as his goal. Ensign collapsed into his seat again as he turned off his violently shaking and smoking vehicle. Those couple minutes of traveling, just shy of a mile, were the most extreme moments Ensign had ever experienced.

8AM: It was eight o'clock in the morning when Ensign finally had enough energy to step from his car and walk up to the pawn shop door. The store was closed. Ensign didn't want to sit in that parking lot and wait for the store to open. Ensign prepared himself to fight his car again.

That drive from Walmart to the pawn shop had burned up his transmission. The Subaru only worked in reverse. Ensign drove backward into the neighborhood behind the pawn shop. He crossed two streets. At the third street, Ensign spun the wheel and lurched back to a stop a hundred feet from the stop sign at the intersection; deep into the neighborhood. The car cut off. Birds chirped in the quiet morning air. The Sun was well into heating up the day.

9AM: Ensign's car was finished. Smoke dissipated from underneath the hood. The smell of burning material was thick in the air. Ensign knew he wasn't going to be driving it any farther than that street in that neighborhood. Ensign emptied out all of the used syringes and garbage drug paraphernalia from one of his safes. He double bagged all of the unneeded drug items and stashed the bag under a seat. Ensign then began sorting out other items from his car. He needed to separate what he wanted to keep, what he wanted to sell, and what he needed to throw away.

10AM: Suddenly, there was a random guy standing right next to Ensign. Question after question, the guy talked incessantly. There were obvious mental deficiencies. Ensign was extremely suspicious. He had never heard anyone fit the stereotypical mental handicap as perfectly as had that guy. Twenty minutes later, the guy walked down the road to the house where he said he lived.

11AM: Police showed up. It had been a bit since Ensign last told his story to the police. Ensign filled in the female officer; up to the part where he was sorting out items to pawn so he could afford a tow.

12PM: The weird guy came back again and asked more questions. Ensign remained busy sorting through items in his car. Ensign's answers became short. His tone became curt. The guy, tired of the interaction, wandered down the road in the direction opposite the house where he said he lived.

1PM: After failing multiple times, Ensign abandoned the idea of making a cart out of floor jacks to pull items to the pawn shop. The wheels were too small. The load was precarious and unstable. He would never be able to pull the floor jacks a quarter mile to the pawn shop. Instead, Ensign unbolted the hood from his Subaru. He tied ratchet straps to the corners of the hood, and he loaded items on top of the improvised sled he made from his car's hood.

2PM: Ensign wrapped the rope around his midsection. In the heat and sunlight, Ensign pulled the hood along behind him through the neighborhood and across the strip of shops facing the main road. The quarter mile of extreme cardio wrecked Ensign physically. A pawn shop employee saw Ensign collapse at the front of the store. She brought Ensign two bottles of cold water. Ensign had trouble drinking the water as he desperately tried to catch his breath, barely on the edge of consciousness.

3PM: The trip was a disappointment. The pawn shop was uninterested in many of the items Ensign had with him on the hood of his car. The shop wanted fun items like his flame thrower and the drone a friend of his gave him back in Detroit, but they didn't buy three quarters of the items Ensign had with him. That meant Ensign didn't make much money. It also meant the weight of the items on the car hood was going to prove to be another challenge to drag the quarter mile back to his car.

4PM: Ensign strapped his gun on his ankle. He put his laptop in his backpack, along with his backup drive, and the very little drugs he had left. He made sure his toiletries, and small items he frequently used, were in his duffle bag. Ensign locked up his car and walked with his backpack and duffle bag back towards the main road to find a restaurant to get some food to eat.

5PM: Ensign sat in the air-conditioned dark of the Jamaican restaurant. He thoroughly enjoyed his meal and drink. It was the first time he had eaten food all day. Ensign appreciated the moment; a relief from all that was going on around him. It was a reprieve from the stress of the day.

6PM: As Ensign turned the corner, his heart dropped. Panic overtook him. No clear thoughts made any sense in his brain. Ensign's car was gone. All of his belongings were gone. Suddenly, Ensign had nothing. He no longer had a place to sleep. He no longer had a home. Ensign had the clothes he was wearing, a backpack, a duffle bag, and a handgun. He was alone, without shelter from the weather and the bugs.

7PM: After a brief conversation with a homeowner down the

street from where his car had last sat, Ensign walked out of the neighborhood. Ensign then walked, with his duffle bag and backpack, the mile back to the Walmart parking lot.

8PM: All the other cars camped in the Walmart parking lot were still parked in the same spaces. The tow truck never came. Samuel's words had instigated Ensign's paranoia, and nothing had come of it for anyone but Ensign; his car and belongings were gone, his home and shelter had disappeared. Ensign's clothes, collectables, electronics, everything… He lost the last of his supply of tadalafil; the drug he used to stay hard when crystal interfered with intimacy. Ensign lost flash drives full of videos and pictures, documented memories from his travels. Ensign lost the letters his mom wrote him over twenty-five years; the letters she gave him before she died. Ensign had them in a safe in his Subaru…and they were gone, along with everything else.

9PM: Ensign walked past Samuel's car. Ensign aggressively confronted Samuel. Soon, he decided it wasn't worth it. Ensign insulted Samuel one last time before walking across the parking lot and down another street.

10PM: Ensign found a gas station with a picnic table behind it. Ensign called Lyla. Ensign knew Lyla from the website. They had been in contact for a few years. They had talked frequently about Ensign coming to be with Lyla in San Antonio, Texas when the time was right.

"Lyla?"

"Hi, baby."

"I think the time is right…"

Over the next hour, the two of them caught up with each other on what was going on in each of their lives. Before the phone conversation ended, Lyla and Ensign reached a mutual conclusion. Ensign was going to be with Lyla in San Antonio.

11PM: Ensign fell asleep for an hour under the night sky as he sat on the picnic table behind the gas station.

12AM: Ensign reached out to Lex. He explained his situation in a text message. A half hour passed by as Ensign remained seated at the picnic table. Ensign's phone notification went off. Lex sent Ensign money for a bus ticket to San Antonio.

1AM: Ensign booked the bus trip. The bus was scheduled to leave at three o'clock the following afternoon. The bus was set to depart from the bus station in downtown Tampa. Ensign texted Lyla the information. He then set up a ride service to pick him up from the Walmart parking lot and drive him to downtown Tampa at six o'clock in the morning.

Ensign, once he finished making arrangements, stood up from the picnic table behind the gas station. He strapped his backpack over his shoulders and picked up his duffle bag. Ensign then walked a quarter mile across the Walmart shopping center, back to the far side where the ride service was scheduled to meet him five hours later.

The Bus Did

With his backpack as a pillow, Ensign laid on the sidewalk at the very end of the strip mall in the Walmart parking lot. The next hours, Ensign spent in contemplation. He couldn't believe he had lost everything. He was tired, both mentally and physically. He knew he wasn't going to sleep anymore that night. All he could do was lean against the bricks of the strip mall and wait on his ride to whisk him away from the parking lot; the place he had called home for the prior month. Ensign had no home. He was sad. 2021; the year, so far, had proven hard to navigate. Life was difficult to manage.

The Sun came up as Ensign gazed out the back window of the car. The driver suddenly realized he was about to miss his exit. He jerked the steering wheel hard and shot across two lanes of traffic, narrowly avoiding the cement barricade at the top of the interstate exit. Ensign didn't even flinch. He didn't care in the least about what was going on in the world outside his head. He continued to gaze to the Tampa skyline. The car took surface streets and made its way to the bus station in downtown Tampa.

It was seven thirty in the morning when Ensign stepped into the bus station. Ensign had almost eight hours ahead of him to wait before he could board his bus to another part of the country. Florida was about to be in Ensign's past. Texas was in his future. Ensign's first ever trip by bus was about to begin later that day. Ensign had time to kill…he had a plan for how to spend his last hours in Tampa, Florida.

Ensign was sore from all the walking he had done the previous day. His backpack and his duffle bag, though he was happy he at least had those items with him, were both heavy items to carry everywhere with him. The straps cut into his neck as he walked. The strain on his back required frequent moments of rest. One block over from the bus station, Ensign found a restaurant.

Ensign took his bags off from around his body and set them in a seat at the only open table in the deli. The restaurant was full. Over half of the customers were police. Ensign left his bags and stepped over to queue up in line. Ensign ordered some food. The lady in line in front of him must have inferred that Ensign was having a difficult day. She bought Ensign his breakfast. Ensign thanked her. He sat down and quietly ate his breakfast at the deli in downtown Tampa.

Feeling full, and as rested as he could possibly feel in his predicament, Ensign slung his bags over his back and stepped out into the already sweltering summer morning. On the approach with the ride service, Ensign had seen row after row of cars as he gazed out the back window on the drive to the bus station; hundreds of cars filling in underneath bridges in any paved sections of downtown Tampa. Ensign had hours to kill. He decided he may as well see if he could find his impounded Subaru and his belongings.

The hours went by painfully. Ensign's neck, back, and feet hurt constantly. The heat of the day was almost unbearable; it radiated from the pavement as he walked up and down the streets downtown. It was a valiant effort, but Ensign never found his car. He stumbled back to the bus station an hour before he was scheduled to leave Florida. Sore and exhausted, he collapsed into a rigid plastic seat inside the bus station.

Ensign listened carefully to make sure he didn't miss his boarding call. He lined up at the proper gate when the announcement came. Ensign handed over his ticket, and he kept his two bags with him when he stepped onto the bus. Sweat poured from Ensign's body as he took a seat near the back of the bus. Once the bus began moving, Ensign removed his tattoo equipment from his backpack. As the bus slowly meandered westward down the highways and byways of the Gulf coast of

Florida, Ensign tattooed eyeballs on the back of his left hand.

Since Ensign hadn't taken a trip by bus before climbing on the bus in Tampa, he didn't know how the trips worked. He didn't know about the scheduled stops and breaks. He didn't know about the bus switches. Ensign didn't know the difference in time between a bus ride and a car trip. The bus was going to be his home on the journey to San Antonio for the next three days.

Bus vibes were weird. Ensign felt an odd sort of comradery with the others on the bus with him. They were all on a cross-country trip together. They had a mission; it would end in the middle of Texas, fifty hours and almost two thousand miles after it began. The driver and all the passengers had the same goal in mind; arrive safely in San Antonio with minimal discomfort and issues.

When the bus stopped at certain gas station parking lots, people got off to smoke, buy food, and use the restroom. When the bus pulled into various bus stations, a person or two would step off, other passengers from the station would take their places on the bus. In Mississippi, everyone was required, along with all their luggage, to vacate the bus. An hour later, another bus arrived in the parking lot to carry everyone the rest of the way to Texas. The stops were frequent, the drive was long, but the seats were surprisingly comfortable. It was a unique and interesting experience. Ensign had never known such a scene prior to that first bus trip.

"Houston, we've had a problem. We've had a main B bus undervolt."

The bus screeched and jerked as the driver applied the brakes when he docked it in downtown Houston. It was the middle of the day, and Ensign could see the heat in the air outside, through the bus windows. Houston was another station where Ensign was to completely switch to another bus. There was a four-hour layover at the downtown Houston station before the next bus was set to arrive and board.

The food kiosks within security boundaries inside the bus station were all closed. Ensign was hungry. He saw a McDonald's restaurant across the street, through the wall of windows of the bus station. Ensign saw the metal detector he would be required to walk through on his way back into the terminal. He paid it no mind. He figured he could easily get his handgun and a bit of drug paraphernalia back inside despite the security search upon his re-entry. Food was more of a concern in that moment; no way was he waiting to eat for four more hours at the station, and however else long he would be on the next bus before the driver stopped for a break.

The heat instantly enveloped Ensign in an uncomfortable embrace. Sweat began to pour off his body everywhere as soon as he stepped outside into the day. It was so bright. Ensign had to squint as he continuously wiped sweat from his brow. Ensign guessed Texas was going to be less humid than Florida. He was wrong. He stepped into a literal urban jungle. The extreme moisture in the air made it ever so much worse than if it just been a dry heat.

The next thing Ensign noticed was the absurd number of people all over downtown Houston. There were people congregated in groups smoking cigarettes. There were shady and shifty characters scurrying about the streets and sidewalks. Makeshift tents and tarps sheltered others from the Sun. There were sleeping derelicts lined up directly on the cement of the sidewalk, lying across the walkway. As Ensign walked towards the McDonald's, he stepped over four sleeping bums in a row. It was like a sort-of homeless hurdles.

Ensign passed by the armed guard in the McDonald's parking lot. At a glance, Ensign wasn't sure if the guy was security or an actual police officer. When he looked again, Ensign saw he was Houston police. The McDonald's lobby wasn't open to the public. Instead, there was a wooden door fastened in place. The door had a hole cut in it. Ensign changed his mind when he saw the setup. He decided not to hand his last few dollars of cash through the door to possibly get food in return. Ensign passed by the officer again as he left the parking lot.

Ensign was sore again. Carrying his bags around his neck and on his back was hurting his back and neck. Ensign took a second to remove the bags at an intersection and set them on the sidewalk for a brief moment to rest. A guy from across the street walked directly up to Ensign as he stood on the corner to rest. The guy began to talk.

"Hey, buddy. Yo, you got like a dollar I can get from you?"

Ensign was instantly mad. His answer conveyed his anger.

"What? Do YOU have a dollar for ME? You probably have more money than me! How about you give me a dollar? Give me a dollar!"

The guy looked bewildered. He hadn't expected Ensign to reply as he had. The guy held up his hand and apologized as he quickly walked away from Ensign and went about his day. Ensign shook it off, and he picked up his bags again. He walked around the block and weaved through the people of downtown Houston. The look on his face from that point until he reached the door to the bus terminal on the other side of the block went a long way to keep anyone else from approaching him to ask him for anything.

As soon as Ensign stepped back into the bus station, he saw that the food kiosks were open for business. He also saw the line ahead of him as people waited to pass through security and the metal detector leading back inside the terminal. The same angry lady was on point as she searched through bags at the metal detector. Ensign waited as the line moved closer to the checkpoint.

Ensign lucked out as he reached the metal detector. The security lady, as soon as Ensign's non-problematic bag reached her, got tossed a question from someone already through the detector. Ensign slid his hot bag through to the other side as he walked through the metal detector. He quickly put his backpack on his shoulders as the security lady was distracted and pointing to something on the other side of the terminal; apparently answering the question of the commuter.

The lady searched through Ensign's other bag as her interaction with the commuter came to an end. Ensign could see in her eyes that she knew something was amiss. She couldn't pinpoint what it was, and she handed Ensign his bag once she finished the search. Ensign walked away from her as he put his duffle bag over the strap to his backpack on his right shoulder. Ensign smiled as he walked across the terminal to the pizza stand.

After all that hassle outside the terminal and coming back inside, Ensign bought a pizza just twenty feet from where he had stepped off the bus two hours prior. After he ate, Ensign patiently waited until his next bus arrived, unloaded, and was then ready to re-board. Ensign smiled as he sank down into his seat on the crowded bus to San Antonio. Ensign recorded video from the window. Houston became smaller behind the departing bus.

Angel Lust

As the bus pulled into downtown San Antonio, Ensign took his phone from his pocket. He sent Lyla a text. The San Antonio bus station occupied a large building in the middle of downtown. Ensign walked through the terminal, and he stepped outside into the hot Texas sunlight. When he found a bench on the sidewalk, Ensign took his bags off of his shoulders and sat down. Again, sweat poured, and Ensign continuously wiped his eyes and face.

Fifteen minutes later, Lyla pulled up in front of the bench. Ensign gathered up his bags and loaded them into the back of Lyla's car. Ensign hopped into the passenger seat of Lyla's PT Cruiser. He looked over at Lyla. She was already smiling as she gazed back at him. Ensign asked a question as he smiled back.

"What?"

"You look exactly as you do online. I'm so happy!"

"Did you think I was catfishing you? We've video talked a hundred times..."

"I'm just happy you are who I hoped you would be. Are you hungry?"

"Absolutely. I haven't eaten since Houston."

"Well, I know a great place to pick up tacos. It's on the way home."

"Bet. That's my favorite food."

Ensign hadn't bathed in a month. He apologized to Lyla for

possibly smelling offensive from the past month he spent in his car. Lyla replied, she told Ensign he smelled fine. She confirmed that he had no smell at all. Ensign had wondered if, after a certain point, the bacteria on skin reaches a homeostasis. He noticed, after the first week of not bathing, that the smell of sweat seemed to disappear. He wasn't sure if he had gotten used to the smell of sweat or if that homeostasis was an actual thing. Lyla confirmed the latter. She told Ensign he could relax while she bathed him once they got back to her house. Lyla also informed Ensign that she owned a massage table.

Freshly bathed and massaged, Ensign began his clean life as a Texas resident. Ensign was clean from drugs as well. He had run out of crystal just before boarding the bus in Tampa earlier in the week. That was about to change, though. Lyla had a crystal habit of her own. Lyla wanted to get high before she had sex with Ensign. A slight smile crept onto Ensign's face when he noticed Lyla was trying to bring up the subject of introducing drugs to their dynamic. Usually, it was Ensign attempting to broach the subject. Ensign welcomed the situation with open arms.

"I thought you'd never ask."

Though it had only been a few days drug free, a wave of relief washed over Ensign when he realized Lyla wanted to do drugs. A bigger wave of relief washed over him when Lyla pulled out a shoe box of supplies from under her bed. Lyla didn't just have the urge to do drugs, she didn't just have the equipment with which to do the drugs, she had the drugs. Lyla's shoe box contained multiple pipes, a few razor blades, a mirror, and no less than four separate bags of crystal.

From the time Ensign ran out of drugs in Florida earlier in the week, he wondered when he would next have the opportunity to get high. The opportunity was there in Lyla's bedroom as the two of them sat naked on Lyla's bed and prepared their works. Lyla loaded an oil burner pipe because her preferred route of administration was smoking. Ensign lined up a big pile of crystal on the mirror using a razor blade. Ensign was going to use another oil burner as a hotrail stem by heating the tube end with a torch and putting the bubble end up to his nostril.

"Watch this."

Lyla's eyes widened and her mouth dropped open slightly as Ensign exhaled the hotrail.

"That's the most smoke I've ever seen…"

"I told ya. Dragon smoke. I'm f'n lit!" Ensign's body began to tingle as he spoke.

"Good. Now, come here. We have bedroom promises to keep to each other."

Lyla was a top. She climbed on top and took Ensign from behind. Ensign felt the firmness of her large silicone breasts against his back as the two of them rhythmically moved together. Ensign was feeling wonderful in the moment. He was happy to be back on crystal again after the multi-day break from the drug. Everything else was inconsequential.

Easy to Play; Difficult to Master

Lyla worked as a volunteer at a local youth center during the weekdays. Thursday through Saturday nights, Lyla worked as a performer at a show bar. Lyla also worked brunch hours at a different show bar each Sunday. Ensign had a lot of time to himself, which he filled with work of his own. Fueled by crystal, Ensign worked around the clock most days. He taught himself as he went. He learned with Lyla's home as his canvas.

For a full month, Ensign gave his all to the task at hand. Lyla bought supplies and gave Ensign freedom to be as creative as he wished within some broad guidelines and stipulations. Ensign had never before remodeled a home, but the time and place was right; Lyla's mobile home in a San Antonio trailer park in the summer of 2021.

The project began outside. In the awful heat and nearly one hundred percent humidity, Ensign swung a hammer into bricks for hours to create the material needed for a rock garden around the entire trailer. The kitchen and dining room were completely remodeled. A floor was replaced in one of the bedrooms and in the living room. Two other bedrooms were combined into one large dressing room/closet. Ensign barely slept. He worked through all hours, day and night. He took breaks to get high and video interact. At the end, Ensign was proud of the work he had done. At the end, Lyla and Ensign were barely on speaking terms. At the end, Lyla bought Ensign a bus ticket.

Ensign thought he had already lost it all. Ensign thought he had been dragging along rock bottom. He wondered when he was going to begin to ascend again. There was something else Ensign failed to even register in his mind. He wasn't at rock bottom. He was at a bottom, for sure, but he wasn't about to ascend anytime soon. Ensign was about to slip from the ledge of that plateau on which he had been scraping along since losing his car in Florida. He was about to be sucked down into the depths of a trench at a new rock bottom; one he hadn't ever imagined existed. Ensign hadn't yet lost everything. He was a fool to think things couldn't get worse.

Bus in Two; Electric Boogaloo

The San Antonio scenery passed by as Ensign gazed out from the passenger side window of Lyla's car. Not much was said on the half-hour ride from Lyla's house to the show bar downtown. It was still light outside, but the sky had that beginning darkness as the evening began. Ensign wasn't focused on anything outside as Lyla drove down the congested interstate highway. It was Ensign's last evening in San Antonio. Ensign's thoughts weighed heavily on him as memories of 2021 played out in his mind. Ensign's eyes began to water. Ensign felt a disbelief for what had become of his life. Texas, like Florida, was about to be behind him. 2021 was only halfway over. Ensign silently sulked as he rode with Lyla on the interstate highway.

Lyla was scheduled to perform two shows at the downtown show bar. Ensign waited in Lyla's car as she went inside the club for two hours. Ensign was fine with the time alone. He cracked the windows in the car, and he thought about life while sitting in that parking lot in downtown San Antonio, Texas. Much had gone wrong. Ensign lost control of his life a while back. He was fine with it when he was at the high points. Those high points had been washed away with the memories of times no longer tangible.

Ensign felt scared as he wondered what came next. Each time he thought things were going to turn around for the better, they somehow managed to become worse. When Ensign thought he had nothing left to lose, he found he was able to lose more. Each time he thought he had nothing left; he was pushed down to a new bottom where he dragged along at the lowest point.

It was ten o'clock at night when Lyla pulled into the parking lot across the street from the bus station. Ensign gathered up his small amount of belongings and stepped from the PT Cruiser. Though happy to be away from the tension he felt anytime he was in Lyla's presence, he suddenly felt fully exposed and vulnerable to the world around him. Again, Ensign was truly homeless. In two hours, he was about to begin another trip across the country.

Like his first bus ride from Florida to Texas, Ensign wasn't going to be in control of anything; not the stops or the route, not the people with him or the time the trip took. Ensign was again putting his faith in fate; he was going to literally be along for the ride. As Ensign stepped from the darkness of the San Antonio night, into the surprisingly crowded bus terminal, he felt he had reached a particularly low point in life. He was alone. He was about to cross the country alone.

Earlier in the week, Ensign took his friend Jane up on an offer which he realized she had made in haste one night after a couple of drinks. Ensign's experience renting a room from Jane when he left his house at the end of 2018 had been a mutually positive situation. Jane had recently offered Ensign a place to stay when he explained to her that his time at Lyla's house in Texas had run its course.

A couple of days later, Ensign wasn't sure Jane's offer stood when he discussed with her how he had a bus ticket to Toledo. In retrospect, Ensign realized Jane had probably invited him back to her house while intoxicated after an evening at the bar. Ensign had no other options in that moment, so he stayed on course and let Jane know to expect him within a week.

Ensign sat in the bus terminal and contemplated all which had gone wrong in Texas. He had again reached a new rock bottom. The steps downward were blatant and clearly visible in retrospect. He found where his car was being held in impound, but he had no means to get back to Florida to recover his belongings. Everything was gone forever; forfeited to a destiny of loss.

Ensign's dynamic with Lyla progressed as had other dynamics

in Ensign's life. Ensign lost interest in intimacy, and he closed off emotionally. Ensign distanced himself and retreated into himself, sleeping in a separate room and avoiding interaction with Lyla by busying himself constantly with the remodeling of Lyla's home. Ensign and Lyla seemed to avoid each other, which was difficult to do inside of a mobile home.

Without a vehicle, Ensign spent all of his time at Lyla's house. There was nowhere within walking distance, in the hot Texas summer, had Ensign wished to get away for a bit to clear his head. Tension and resentment built on both sides of the dynamic. The month Ensign spent in San Antonio felt so much longer. While stranded in his car in Florida, Ensign still felt a sense of freedom. In Texas, Ensign felt all he did was at the mercy of another. Ensign kept his head down, and he focused on his work on the house. Despite feeling lost and alone, Ensign felt some relief as he sat at the bus terminal and waited to begin yet another chapter of his life.

Ensign thought of something else as he sat at the bus terminal in downtown San Antonio. Ensign had one twenty-ounce bottle of water with him. That was fine; he could keep it and refill it at different stops along the way. Ensign had two granola bars with him. That was all the food he had. Ensign also had no money at all. Ensign had two granola bars.

The bus trip, with all stops and layovers, was going to take four days. Ensign knew he was in a bad spot with regard to food. What he didn't know was how things were going to be worse than he could have ever imagined...far worse. Ensign thought his second bus trip across the country was going to progress without incident. Ensign, already at a low point, figured he was due for some good fortune. He had no idea how much farther down he could go. 2021 had shown Ensign hardship and tribulation...and Ensign hadn't seen anything yet.

Vast Difference

Ensign jerked awake. Five minutes later, Ensign's thoughts came online. The events of the previous five minutes played out in Ensign's brain. Ensign's eyes opened wide, and his jaw dropped open. Ensign ran. Ensign ran from the bathroom. He ran through the store. Ensign ran out into the parking lot and froze. The parking lot was empty.

"Oh, no! NO!"

The Sun was just beginning to rise. Ensign stared across the parking lot; eyes wide and jaw hanging open. By leaps and bounds, Ensign's life had instantly become much, much worse. Ensign never imagined that moment even being a possibility. Ensign had sat in pity for himself back at the bus terminal in San Antonio three days earlier. He thought he had it bad while he was still in Texas. He never imagined the possibility, which then became his reality, three days down the road.

Ensign replayed the events of the previous five minutes as he frantically searched for a phone number in his phone. Those prior events played out, step by step, like a horror movie in Ensign's brain. Though his thoughts were all over the place, those previous five minutes of activity were clear and concise; it was as if fate were taunting Ensign with clarity and awareness.

-Ensign jerked awake; it had been the sound of the bus, as it stopped in the parking lot of a Love's truck stop in central Illinois, which woke him up.

-Due to exhaustion, Ensign acted without thinking when he awoke to the bus's brakes.

-The situation failed to register since Ensign was barely awake; he wasn't at a scheduled bus stop, but rather a short stop for just the driver to exit the bus early in the morning.

-Ensign grabbed his bag, he pushed past the gate on the bus, and he wandered into the bathroom at the truck stop. Nobody else from the bus was inside the truck stop.

-As Ensign sat in the bathroom, the realization that he had just messed up hit him the second he was awake enough to comprehend his situation. That was when he ran from the bathroom.

The driver of that bus had taken over somewhere in the Midwest a day prior. She was a stern older woman who specifically mentioned multiple times that she wasn't going to wait for anyone at stops. She absolutely proved her point that morning in Kankakee, Illinois. To make matters worse, she had forced Ensign to store his duffle bag in a compartment underneath the bus earlier, when it first departed. She told Ensign he was alright with the backpack, but the duffle bag was too large for the seats. It was the first time Ensign was made to check either of his bags. The bus had left Ensign in the dust...and it had taken his duffle bag to Chicago without him.

Ensign was hungry. He hadn't eaten since that last granola bar two days prior. In that moment, Ensign didn't care about that. He tried and tried, but he could not reach anyone to get in contact with that bus driver. Though he had already lost everything before that morning, he somehow managed to lose half of the nothing he had hung onto. Again, he reached a new low; one which he hadn't thought possible until it happened. Ensign was alone in the middle of nowhere with nothing; no food, no money, no transportation, and no plan to survive the day.

Ensign's duffle bag had been full of what little he had left to his name; toiletries, some clothes Lyla bought him in Texas, a digital scale which doubled as a power bank for charging his cell phone, some various adult novelties which managed to outlast the loss of his car, his old, expired driver's license, and a container of foot powder. The container of foot powder had something inside it: Ensign had placed a small plastic bag in it prior to beginning the bus trip from Texas to Ohio. The plastic bag had almost an eightball of crystal inside of it. Ensign's duffle bag was gone.

Ensign still had his backpack. Fortunately, other items weren't lost when the bus left him in the middle of Illinois. Ensign's backpack had his laptop, his phone, his tattoo equipment, his handgun, and a glass oil burner. The pipe had a melted gram of crystal inside of it. Ensign still had drugs. Ensign walked back inside the truck stop. He locked himself in a stall in the bathroom and pulled out the oil burner. Ensign heated the glass bubble with a small torch, and he got high on crystal as he attempted to evaluate his current situation. Ensign was in trouble, and he knew it.

Kankakee, Illinois wasn't a big city at all. It was a rundown town in the middle of Midwest farmland. That meant there wasn't even a real bus terminal. Ensign sorted out the situation, and he received some information on how to proceed. The "bus station" was ran from a seedy hotel across the city. The "bus station" was closed until mid-day. There was a local route that the city buses circled. The first bus was due to stop by the bus stop a quarter mile down the road from the truck stop in forty-five minutes. Ensign packed up his drug paraphernalia and began to walk. He needed to get on the local bus so he could get to the bus hotel across the city when it opened later in the day.

Ensign also began the frustrating and arduous process of reaching customer service for the bus line, explaining his situation, and being put on another bus to Chicago. Ensign realized something else in that moment; once in Chicago, he will already have missed his next bus to Toledo. Ensign put that dilemma on the backburner, and he focused on guaranteeing a bus from the middle of nowhere.

As Ensign rode local buses around the city, as he randomly got off at bus stops in various locations to walk around, he began to sort out his situation with the bus line. Ensign had to speak with multiple people to try to find who could secure him a trip from Kankakee to Chicago. Frustration built as Ensign repeated his story to each person with whom he was next connected. Ensign hated everything about that morning in that city where he had been dropped. Ensign hated being hungry.

Ensign hated when customer service wasn't sure if he had been left behind or kicked off the bus due to bad behavior. He hated circling the city with nowhere to go. He hated being yelled at by some redneck lady for not wearing a mask on one of the local buses around the city. He hated being told that the only bus out of Kankakee to Chicago wasn't until six o'clock in the evening. Ensign hated life as he wandered through shady places and did his best to avoid interactions with shady people.

The hotel, which doubled as a bus stop in the evenings, also doubled as a den of drugs and prostitution. Ensign spent most of the afternoon watching customers and suppliers go in and out of various rooms at the rundown hotel. Ensign was thankful he had his handgun. He fully expected someone to try to separate him from his backpack, but that situation never materialized.

Ensign's next bus, the bus to Chicago, showed up forty-five minutes late. At seven o'clock in the evening, twelve hours after being left in Kankakee, Ensign departed from the hotel in the middle of nowhere. He settled in for the next couple of hours. Ensign had new bus tickets. They were confusing to him, but he figured he knew where to get off and where to board the next bus in Chicago. Yes...he knew which stop.

Goonin'

Well...Ensign had a fifty-fifty shot at it. He knew it was the current terminal or the next one. Both were in downtown Chicago. Ensign knew he needed to be at the main terminal downtown. With the bus stopping at what appeared to be a main terminal, Ensign grabbed his bag and stepped off with ten other people.

Ensign looked around through the throng. The bus pulled away from the stop. It joined the traffic pattern with multiple other buses, pulling out into the congested Chicago city traffic. People were everywhere. It was the opposite of the scene in Kankakee. Ensign began to realize a terrible fact as he wandered through the sea of pedestrians; though he was for sure in Chicago, he had gotten off at the wrong bus terminal. A whole new world of problems opened up for Ensign that evening in downtown Chicago.

For a half hour, Ensign split his time between reading bus maps on the walls in the outside heat of summer and wandering through the underground terminal to find anyone who could help him find his bearings. At the bottom of some cement steps, there was a metal cage-style gate which led into the Chicago subway system. Guarding the gate was a female Chicago police officer. As he had done many times on the phone earlier, Ensign told his story to the officer. The officer took pity on Ensign.

Since Ensign had no money, the officer bought him an all-expenses-paid trip on the Chicago subway. She even took the time to write down the three locations where he needed to switch trains. The officer explained where Ensign's subway journey was going to end and then where he would need to walk to reach the main bus terminal in another part of downtown Chicago. Ensign almost cried as he thanked the officer for her help. She wished him luck as he headed through the metal gates and into the massive and crowded subway system of Chicago, Illinois.

After the train rides and the multi-block walk through downtown, Ensign waited in a line inside the main Chicago bus terminal. Once Ensign reached the worker at the front of the line, he again told his story. It was already past the time his connecting bus to Ohio had departed the station. Ensign needed to find his duffle bag and secure a new trip to Ohio.

He secured a new trip. Ensign found out he was about to spend the night in the bus terminal in downtown Chicago. His new bus was scheduled to arrive at six o'clock in the morning. Ensign's duffle bag was not recovered in Chicago. Employees suggested it could be waiting for him when he reached Toledo. Ensign doubted he would ever see it again.

Ensign settled in at the crowded bus terminal. The metal seats were too uncomfortable for him to sleep. The noise from the crowd in the bus station was excessive. On two separate occasions through the course of the night, police had to break up fist fights amongst the commuters in the terminal. Ensign knew he wasn't going to sleep, so he locked himself in a bathroom stall and smoked crystal for a short while. Ensign carefully blew the smoke into a handful of toilet paper after each hit, and he felt chemically refreshed from the drug consumption.

At six o'clock the next morning, Ensign took his place in the proper line to wait to board the bus to Toledo. A half an hour later, Ensign was on a seat in the back of the bus. That bus, unlike all the previous buses, was only half full. Ensign was the only person in the back half of the bus. It was a relief to have some room to himself. He was on the last bus of his multi-state trip from the bottom to the top of the country, and he had just a few hours before he would arrive in Ohio.

Ensign engaged with one of the females from the website

between Chicago and Gary, Indiana. The two of them had shared a sexual dynamic during the previous three years. As the two of them interacted, Ensign considered the fact that he was the only person in the back half of the bus. The woman encouraged Ensign to act on it. Ensign complied. As the bus passed from Illinois to Indiana, Ensign recorded video as he used his hand to climax while he sat on the bus. Ensign sent the video. It was met with approval.

Ensign cleaned himself up and sat back for the remainder of the bus trip. It had been almost a week since he left Texas. Ensign was hungry, frustrated, and exhausted. He was stressed from the events along the way. He was worried about his missing duffle bag, and he was worried for what was about to become his life the moment he stepped from the bus in Toledo.

When he left the Midwest at the beginning of the year, Ensign was full of hope and optimism. On his return, he was broken; he had lost his vehicle, his home, and almost all of his belongings with which he traveled the country. He had lost his freedom to go where he wanted when he wanted, to do what he wished when he wished. He had lost all his money, and he was again almost out of drugs. Ensign was in a bad spot, and he no longer looked forward to the future. Instead, he feared more bad luck. Each time he thought he had hit rock bottom; he somehow went down lower. Ensign was scared to think of what could be lower than his current situation. He learned he was never truly at rock bottom. Though in that moment he couldn't imagine how, he knew things could always get worse. That much had been proven multiple times.

Lifetimes Ago

The familiar scenery outside the window of the bus weighed heavily on Ensign's mind. A sense of sadness and defeat washed over Ensign as the bus made its way down Broadway in south Toledo. Though the scenery was familiar from a life long gone, the situation was new. Ensign remembered being in the car with his parents and sister as they drove down Broadway when Ensign was a child. Ensign's grandparents, his father's parents, lived on a street four miles away from the Toledo bus terminal. Their house, where Ensign's father was raised, was visible from Broadway. Holidays were spent with Ensign's extended family at that house near the other end of Broadway in Toledo.

Ensign was alone on the bus as it pulled into the terminal on that sweltering summer day in Toledo, Ohio. As Ensign thought back to his childhood, he felt memories of a life with which he no longer had any connection. Ensign's mom had died ten years prior. Except for that time Ensign stopped at his dad's house before he left for Florida at the beginning of 2021, Ensign had no interaction with his father in the years prior. Ensign last spoke with his sister back in 2020, while he was in Colorado. She had her own life hundreds of miles away from Ohio.

Though Ensign's grandfather on his dad's side had passed away, Ensign guessed that his grandmother still lived four miles away; at the other end of Broadway in south Toledo. Ensign thought about what he was going to do as the bus unloaded, and he stepped into the terminal. His first order of business was to again attempt to recover his duffle bag of belongings. Once he thought beyond that task, Ensign came to a conclusion; he had no other immediate option but to walk the four miles through south Toledo to his grandmother's house.

As Ensign had assumed, his bag was not at the Toledo terminal. It hadn't made it to Ohio to await his arrival. There was no sign of it anywhere. The Toledo terminal contacted the Chicago station; it still hadn't shown up there. Toledo took Ensign's information, and the manager of the bus station assured Ensign that he would contact him if it showed up. Ensign knew he wouldn't be hearing from them. He knew his bag was gone forever. Later, he figured he would have to make a complaint to the bus company.

Ensign, with backpack on his shoulders and handgun strapped to the shoulder strap of the backpack, stepped out into the hot sunlight in south Toledo. He began to walk. He was sore and tired, hungry and depressed. As sweat dripped into his eyes and soaked his clothing, Ensign mentally prepared for a four mile walk in the heat of summer. He had no other option; he walked. The scenery, though familiar, was completely different. The buildings he had seen so many times before, they all seemed foreign to him. For the next couple of hours, Ensign walked down a street which he had been down many times before, but never in the way he existed in that moment. His old life was long gone. His current life was precarious and uncertain. He walked.

Around the corner of the cross-street, right before the viaduct, the house still looked as it had lifetimes ago. The front porch was glassed in. Ensign was probably around ten years old when the porch was enclosed. There were three cement steps leading up to the thin glass door on the front of the porch. Ensign stepped up and knocked on the door. He waited. He didn't see any movement inside. He knocked again. That time, the knocking elicited a response from inside the house.

Ensign hadn't seen his grandmother in years. He was slightly surprised to see her approaching the door on an electric scooter. The surprise wore off fast; she had always been a larger woman. The scooter made sense. Ensign smiled as his grandma unlocked the door and pushed it open. Ensign, having no clue if he was close to recognizable, spoke to that effect.

"Hi Grandma, it's Ensign; Joe and Marie's son."

Upon receipt of those words, recognition crossed Ensign's grandmother's face. She smiled at her grandson. She invited Ensign inside. Ensign was thankful for the hospitality. Soaked in sweat and exhausted, Ensign collapsed on the floor next to a chair in the living room; his backpack dropped alongside the chair. Observing Ensign's current state, his grandmother offered him food. She told him of items in the kitchen refrigerator. Though Ensign was exhausted from the walk in the heat, his hunger far outweighed his exhaustion. He quickly headed to the kitchen.

Back on the floor in the living room, halfway through his second sandwich, someone walked in the front door. It was Ensign's aunt. Ensign waved as he chugged down a glass of juice. Ensign's aunt and uncle lived a few houses down from his grandma. Ensign's uncle was at work, but his aunt stopped by after grandma called to let her know that Ensign was there. Ensign saw relief in his aunt's eyes when she recognized him. She had stopped over to be sure that it really was Ensign who showed up out of nowhere that summer day in 2021.

Another half of a sandwich, a bowl of chips, and a second glass of juice later; Ensign's aunt stood up to head back home. She was happy Ensign was alright after his recent ordeal, and she was glad to see him again after years apart. The two of them hugged, and Ensign's aunt told him that she hoped to see him again soon. She let Ensign know one more thing on her way out the door.

"I let your uncle Rich know you were here. He told me to tell you he will be over once he's off work. Love ya."

Once Ensign's focus returned to his grandma, he saw she was on the phone. The land line phone was on a table, next to a lamp in the opposite corner of the living room. Grandma, still seated in her scooter, had the phone up to her ear. It only took a few seconds before Ensign knew who was on the other end of the phone. Ensign's grandma then spoke a sentence into the phone which confirmed Ensign had been correct in his assumption.

"Joey, he doesn't have anything…"

Ensign's mood switched. He knew what was being discussed, and he knew he had been right about something back in January when he stopped over at his dad's house on his way to Florida. Ensign had no agenda back then, and he had no agenda as he sat on his grandma's living room floor months later. Ensign was tired, exhausted, and lost. He knew he had been within walking distance when he departed the bus station in Toledo earlier that afternoon. Ensign had no other options. He decided to stop over at his grandma's house.

In the moment he heard his grandma speaking with his dad on the phone, Ensign knew his dad was not anymore connected to his life in any way. Ensign had seen disappointment in his dad's face back in January. He felt disappointment in his own heart that summer day as he sat on the floor at his grandma's house. Ensign hadn't asked his grandma for anything, but he knew his dad was on the phone with her, telling her not to give him anything. Ensign saw his grandma reach the phone out to him. Ensign stood up and walked over to take the phone from her.

"I'm not here trying to get money. I had nowhere else to go."

"What happened? You said you were on your way to Florida."

As Ensign had done many times in the previous couple of days, he told his story. Ensign spoke of what had happened since January. Ensign explained hardships and disappointment. He conveyed the details of his journey to that point in 2021. He also spoke of the positives, such as his discovered ability for home renovation, which he put to work successfully in Texas.

Ensign's dad, as figured, remained stuck on the point that Ensign needed to get a job. Ensign expressed that he understood, but what happened had happened. There was no changing the past, and job advice for the future wasn't going to fix his current situation. Ensign knew his dad had zero insight into his life and who he was as a person. The conversation went in a direction which showed Ensign that his dad was done with him in this life.

"Do not ask your grandma for money."

"What are you talking about? I told you I don't want anything from her." Ensign turned to face his grandma. He spoke to her. "Grandma, I don't want anything from you."

The phone conversation ended. Ensign hung up the phone. He knew his thoughts back in January had been accurate. That conversation confirmed it. Ensign's mom was long gone. His dad was long gone as well.

"Sorry about that, grandma. I seriously don't want anything from you."

"It's ok, hon. Rich should be able to give you a ride wherever you need to go once he gets home from work."

A half hour later, Ensign's uncle Rich walked into the house. Rich and Ensign hugged. The two of them caught up for a bit. Rich offered to give Ensign a ride. He accepted the offer. Ensign had an idea. Ensign's uncle insisted that Ensign take the cash he had on him; forty dollars. Ensign accepted the money and thanked his uncle for the help. After Ensign hugged his grandma goodbye for the last time, he hopped into Rich's car. The two of them hit the road.

"So, where am I takin' ya?"

"Head to Perrysburg."

Ensign felt a lump form in his throat. He typed out a text message. He knew the situation wasn't ideal, but he had no other option. Yes, Jane had previously told Ensign he was welcome to come stay with her again. Ensign knew, deep down, that

Jane had only made that offer on a superficial level. He wasn't comfortable making good on the offer...but it was all he had.

Surface Knowledge and Delusions

Amongst the gridded country roads, crisscrossing the farm fields on the outskirts of Perrysburg, Ensign was again back at Jane's house. The scene in summer of 2021 was a far cry from his experience in the winter of 2018/2019. Ensign had no room of his own; he slept on the couch. Without a car, Ensign no longer came and went as he pleased. No longer being immersed in the drug game, Ensign had no money, and no money was coming in. Ensign's life had come full circle; flushed down a death spiral. Life, in the same place, was so much different.

Three quarters of a mile down one road, a right turn, and another mile down another road was the entrance to Ensign's storage unit complex. The road, the first road from Jane's house, had only fields of crops along the way. The second road, once past the railroad tracks and police station, had more fields with random warehousing and industry on both sides. The speed limits on both of the roads were fifty-five miles per hour.

Traffic was sparse on the first country road, the road leading from Jane's house. Traffic was heavy on the second road leading to the storage complex; it was the main thoroughfare between Perrysburg and smaller rural cities to the east of the metro Toledo area. There were deep runoffs and ditches running alongside the roads. There were crops, mostly corn and soybeans, in the fields; fields which were cut into square grids by the country roads.

The walk back and forth was unpleasant; the heat from the pavement burnt the bottoms of Ensign's shoes. Due to traffic, especially on that second road, much of the walking was spent navigating the uneven gravel and bumpy ground between the pavement and the steep drop-offs into the ditches. The excursions were further complicated by anything Ensign carried with him, either to, or from his storage unit.

Jane worked every day; she already seemed put out by Ensign's presence. Ensign never asked for a ride. He chose to walk each time he felt the need to visit the storage unit. Ensign spent many hours of each visit sorting through his storage unit in an attempt to locate items of need and items he could sell for any sort of money. His time at the storage unit was also a relief from the tension he felt. Tension was building the longer he remained at Jane's house.

On a hot summer day in the first week of July, Ensign's shoes wore out from all the walking through the farmland on the outskirts of Perrysburg. By late afternoon, he had walked close to fifteen miles that day. As he walked back towards Jane's house, down the busy road from his storage unit, a police cruiser pulled up and stopped in front of him. After a brief conversation, Ensign hopped in the cruiser and took a ride another mile down the road, into the city limits of Perrysburg. The fields around him were replaced with strip malls and the large stores of the city. Ensign thanked the officer for the ride and got back to walking again.

Ensign came across the parking lot of the Kroger grocery store. He had a few dollars, so he walked into the store and bought a small box of fried chicken. Instead of then walking the two miles back to Jane's house, he decided to rest on a picnic table outside of the store and eat the chicken.

As he sat and ate, Ensign noticed his ex-wife walking from her car to the store. Ensign didn't say anything as she walked inside. It was the first time he had seen her in years. He was happy to see she looked well. Moments later, she left the store and walked back to her car. Again, Ensign said nothing. She drove away. She hadn't noticed him. Ensign sat and ate the rest of his chicken. He threw away the box once he finished eating.

Ensign walked around to the other side of the Kroger entrance. He bought a cigar from the gas station on the side of the Kroger. He sat at the picnic table between the gas station and the store entrance. Ensign lit the cigar. It was the first Ensign had used any tobacco since back when he began using crystal meth. Since he was no longer on crystal, the desire to use tobacco had returned.

Ensign squinted his eyes. Was that Jane? He saw the silver car pull up and stop at the curb in front of the store. Was Jane there to pick him up and give him a ride back to her house? He saw the blonde ponytail, worn on top of the driver's head, exactly the way Jane wore her hair. It had to be her. Ensign could see that he was being waved over to the car. It was her. He was saved. He didn't have to walk two more miles in the heat to get back to Jane's house. He was rescued.

Ensign reached for the door handle of the car. That was when he saw it. The car wasn't Jane's car. The driver of the car was not Jane. What was going on? Confused, Ensign leaned down to look into the open passenger window of the car. The driver of the car was a pretty, blonde-haired girl in her early twenties. Ensign began the exchange of words.

"Oh, man. I thought you were my friend Jane. You have the same car. Your hair looks exactly like hers…"

The girl was intoxicated on something, Ensign could see it before she even replied. "Is there an ice cream place around here? I'm supposed to meet some friends at an ice cream place around here."

"That's why you waved me over? I thought you were my friend; here to pick me up."

The conversation progressed. A moment later, Ensign was in the passenger seat of Alyssa's car, thanking her for giving him a ride. The situation blew Ensign's mind; a girl who looked just like Jane, in a car which looked just like Jane's car, had motioned him over to her car. Ensign was then riding with a complete stranger back to Jane's house; the same thing he would have been doing if it were actually Jane who stopped to pick him up at Kroger.

Alyssa pulled into Jane's driveway. Jane pulled up right after Alyssa, and she waited in her matching car in the street while Ensign and Alyssa exchanged phone numbers. Alyssa did drugs, as Ensign assumed upon first speaking with her. Alyssa did drugs, and the two of them planned to hang out in the near future. Ensign thanked Alyssa for the ride, and he looked at Jane as he stepped back from Alyssa's car. Jane looked annoyed that she had to wait to pull into her own driveway. Alyssa pulled out to leave, and Jane pulled in her driveway to park.

"Who was that? She was messed up. I was behind you guys the whole way down the road, and she was swerving all over the place."

"Her name's Alyssa. I just met her. I wouldn't have even met her if I hadn't thought it was you. That was so weird."

Evergreen

There was a time when people would drop money on the table in front of Ensign just to be in the presence of his silver serving tray. Like a game of poker, there was a buy-in to sit at the table as Ensign lined up hotrails to keep his friends zooted. After each round, people kicked in again if they wanted the tray passed to them on the next go. That dynamic wasn't an everyday occurrence, but the method had its place in Ensign's game. It all depended on factors such as where he was and who was with him.

It was back in Lansing when that situation became a method naturally; one day, some friends showed up while Ensign was doing hotrails with Dan. They began dropping twenties on the table as the tray went around the circle. Ensign tweaked out the rules for the rest of the sessions as that instance progressed through the evening. Eventually, the sessions were preplanned, and by invitation only.

When the right situation presented, Ensign let his friends know how the next few hours were going to go. Ensign's selected friends learned the drill. Wherever they were, someone made sure the doors were locked. People turned off their phones. Everyone sat in a circle around a table. The money for the first round was passed to Ensign. He pocketed the collection from everyone who was in on the round. The tray went around the table, one person at a time. Ensign heated the glass stem for whomever was on the left of the previous person in the round; a new line of crystal on the tray for their hotrail.

Once the round was complete, Ensign set up another hotrail for himself. Ensign asked who was in on the next round, and the process began again. Money was collected, hotrails were prepared and passed to the left, to the next person in the circle. Some sessions only lasted a round or two; others went on all night. Ensign found those pay-to-play sessions a productive way to hang out and make money at the same time. It was convenient and lucrative, a stress-free good time.

It was a situation Ensign took for granted back when he was on top. It was a scene lost to the past; a scene where just a single repeat of one of those evenings would have been life-changing in mid-2021. Instead, Ensign had no money, no drugs, no car, and no hope. On top of that, Ensign had just received a text message from Jane. It was a message he had expected during the week he was sleeping on her couch. He stared at the words on the screen of his phone as he sat alone in Jane's living room. Jane was back at work after her lunch break that afternoon. Since Jane had stopped back at her house that day for lunch, Ensign had been waiting for it; he could tell. Then, the message came through.

"Dude, I'm sorry. You have to go."

Ensign met Jacob at work back in 2004. During the following five years, the two of them became close friends while working together. When Ensign married his second wife a couple years after he was no longer employed with that company, Jacob was a groomsman in the wedding. Ensign's friendship with Jacob, as with his other dynamics from his earlier life, was put on the back burner when Ensign's life changed in 2018.

Jacob was an interesting character. He trained in martial arts, and he put that training into practice in Ensign's presence. Though Ensign wasn't violent, Jacob was. Ensign had seen Jacob drop multiple people on multiple occasions. Ensign had seen Jacob take on three guys and win. Jacob was a small guy; he was five feet eight and weighed only a hundred and fifty pounds. His size didn't seem to matter when he engaged in fighting.

Jacob, since well before his friendship with Ensign, was also involved in professional wrestling. Back in 2007, Jacob was involved with the Midwest Wrestling Federation. Ensign tagged along with Jacob to a show one night, and he ended up wrestling as a tag team partner for Jacob's match. After the match, Ensign watched Jacob stand up to a bigtime name in televised professional wrestling.

The wrestler, six foot five and two hundred ninety pounds, took issue to the way the match had gone. In the basement of the venue, the wrestler confronted Jacob. He pushed Jacob as he expressed his displeasure. Jacob ran at him. Jacob jumped and pushed the wrestler back. The wrestler was frozen in disbelief when Jacob stood up to him. The two of them cooled off, and the situation resulted in mutual respect. The situation could have gone south fast, but it worked itself out. Jacob wasn't afraid of anyone.

Ensign made a phone call. Jacob and Ensign had been in random communication while Ensign traveled the country, but Ensign's focus was on travel, new dynamics, and drugs. When Ensign returned to northwest Ohio in the summer of 2021, he reached out to Jacob. When Jane gave Ensign the boot, Ensign reached out to Jacob again.

Ensign needed help, and Jacob offered to come pick him up from Jane's house in Perrysburg. Jacob showed up to Jane's house before Jane got back from work that afternoon. Ensign grabbed his belongings. Jacob helped Ensign carry a couple of his bags out to the car.

Though Ensign was close with Jacob, he knew Jacob wasn't right in the head. Ensign had always listened as Jacob went on about all sorts of delusions of grandeur. Upon reconnection in the summer of 2021, Ensign listened as Jacob picked up where he left off. As Jacob drove the two of them from Perrysburg to Toledo, the familiar diatribe flowed from Jacob's mouth. Ensign sat back and listened. He didn't have the energy to add to the conversation.

Three tumultuous days went by as Ensign stayed with Jacob. The two of them took trips to pawn shops so Ensign could attempt to sell items from his storage unit. Ensign managed to make enough money to have his storage unit bill paid for the next month and the unit subsequentially unlocked again so Ensign could regain access. Ensign sorted out more items for sale. The pawn shops around Toledo weren't biting. Ensign tattooed his hand in Jacob's basement while Jacob argued with his sister and parents, upstairs in the house. Ensign slept two nights in Jacob's car as it was parked in the street in front of Jacob's house. The entire situation was stressful. Ensign knew he needed to figure out something else. Jacob's mental state, as always, was very unstable. Jacob's moods switched instantly and frequently. Jacob was unpredictable and slipping farther off the deep end of sanity.

On that third day with Jacob, Ensign knew his time was done. The two of them had returned to west Toledo after Ensign rode along to a metro park on the Maumee River where Jacob "needed" to test out his new electric skateboard. The skateboard arrived that morning at Jacob's house; much to Jacob's delight. Though Ensign tried his best to understand the importance of the skateboard to Jacob's plans of infamy, he only understood two points of the diatribe Jacob spewed to him on the ride: the skateboard was somehow going to complete Jacob's martial arts training, and that was going to lead Jacob to internet domination.

Jacob didn't even use crystal. Ensign could only imagine what would happen if he ever tried it. Ensign had no crystal. Had he; he would never have let Jacob in on it. Jacob's mental state had no place for added stimulation from any form of uppers.

As Jacob drove Ensign and two suitcases' worth of belongings down Alexis Road in west Toledo, his mood instantly changed to aggressive and confrontational. It came out of nowhere. The two of them had been talking peacefully as they rode in the car back towards Jacob's house. Suddenly, Ensign realized Jacob's paranoid delusions were in control. As Jacob began yelling about kicking Ensign out of the car, Ensign calmly thanked Jacob for helping him out over the prior three days. Ensign tried to diffuse the situation, but Jacob continued to become angrier and more irrational. Ensign guessed what was coming before it happened. He knew Jacob would never be violent towards him, but he also knew Jacob had reached his limit.

"I'll kick you out right here if you say that to me again!"

"I love you, man. I appreciate your help. If you want me to, I'll get out."

"I mean it! If you keep saying that…"

"Seriously dude…thanks for your help. If that's what you want to do, it's ok."

Jacob took a right, onto a side street on the north side of Alexis Road. He pulled to a stop across the street from the General Motors Powertrain factory in the middle of the west Toledo area. Jacob stomped his foot down on the brake pedal. His car screeched to a halt. Jacob, with wide unblinking eyes, turned his head to stare at Ensign from the driver's seat of his car. Ensign gazed back to Jacob from the opposite side of the car. After five tense seconds of silence, Ensign spoke.

"As I said, I sincerely thank you for your help. I'm fine here. I love ya, man. I wish you the best."

Jacob sat and stared as Ensign stepped to the ground and opened the back car door to grab his two suitcases. Jacob hopped out from his side and walked around the car to face Ensign. The two of them hugged briefly and Jacob spoke once more before he got back in his car and left Ensign in the middle of west Toledo.

"I…love ya too, man. I hope things work out for you. You just can't be talking like that."

Ensign stood in the road in a random neighborhood across the street from the auto plant, and he watched as Jacob drove away. Ensign, with a suitcase handle in each hand, began to walk into the neighborhood and away from the main road. Sweat poured from him as he began to drag the heavy luggage down the road. Ensign made it fifty feet into the neighborhood. A wheel on his larger, and much heavier, suitcase snapped off at the base. Ensign's belongings weighed too much for the wheel. All it took was fifty feet for the wheel to break, leaving Ensign in an unfamiliar neighborhood, unable to go any farther.

It was afternoon in summer. Ensign was exhausted, hot, and defeated. He pulled his two suitcases up onto the grass beyond the curb, and he collapsed next to them. As sweat poured down his face, Ensign laid back and gave up. He had nowhere to go and no way to get there. As he lay on his back in the grass in that neighborhood, he didn't even have the energy to care.

Cliches, After School Specials, and Free Candy

A half hour passed, then an hour. Clouds came in, and rain began to sprinkle down from the sky. Ensign sat up in the grass in the center median where the roads split off into three directions of streets; lined with houses. The rain continued, but it remained light as the afternoon grew later. Then, like something out of a made for tv movie, a scene played out in real life which Ensign never considered. Outside of lore and urban legend, Ensign had never heard of it in an actual real-world instance.

As Ensign sat there in the grass where the neighborhood streets converged, he adjusted his hand, giving him a firm grip on the gun in his front pocket. The windowless white van pulled up on the street in front of him. Ensign took in the details of the vehicle as it came to a stop at the intersection in the neighborhood. There were no windows on the side of the van behind the driver's window. The van was full-sized and older. It was white, with some rust and missing paint. Two metal ladders were strapped onto the roof. Smoke escaped from the van's exhaust as it sat and loudly idled.

Ensign couldn't see into the driver's window. Though it wasn't sunny outside, the angle of the light, as it reflected on the glass, obscured view of anyone inside. Ensign felt his heartbeat increase. He didn't stand up, but he sat at full attention as he faced the van directly. He felt sweat on his hand as he held his handgun in his pocket. Ensign watched, and the driver's window rolled down. Ensign could see at least two people in the front seats of the white van. Neither had shirts. Both had full beards. Ensign continued to watch. The driver of the van turned to Ensign and spoke.

"Hey!"

Ensign stared at the van. He didn't reply. He didn't move. Short, tense seconds seemed to pass in slow motion. The driver spoke again.

"Hey!"

As Ensign considered how to respond, the driver of the van leaned farther out of his window, staring directly into Ensign's eyes.

"Do you wanna work?"

That sentence caught Ensign off guard. As the words reached his ears, he had to consider the question. Ensign rearranged his thought process. He thought on the question for only a split second before he replied. Ensign yelled one word back across the street to those strangers in the windowless van, a van where he then saw at least three people inside.

"Yes."

"Well, grab your stuff and come on. Jesse will help you load your suitcases in the back on the other side. We gotta hurry. It's supposed to rain hard in a few hours."

Against every bit of childhood advice ever spoken about stranger danger, not taking rides from strangers…and windowless vans, Ensign stood up and dragged his luggage across the street. Between the light rain and his own sweat, Ensign was soaked. Ensign passed his two suitcases up to the man in the back of the van, the only of the three wearing a shirt and not sporting a beard. Ensign climbed in the side door and sat on a bucket amongst the tools and equipment which filled the back of the van. Ensign had surprised himself with how quickly he happily accepted the offer from the three van guys. He was no longer stranded on the side of the road in the summer rain. He suddenly had the chance to earn some much-needed cash. He had something to do for the evening, and he was ready for whatever that entailed.

For the next five hours, Ensign worked alongside the three van guys as they roofed a house on the opposite side of Toledo. Ensign took instruction as he went, being unfamiliar with the process. The men were in a race, against night and the weather, to finish the job they had been working for the previous week. Ensign learned how to hold shingles as they were nailed in place. He carried supplies up and down a ladder at the base of the steep roof. He threw debris from the roof, and he gathered up piles of old roof to carry to the dumpster in the driveway.

Ensign worked hard that evening. The opportunity was a blessing, and Ensign did his best to keep up. He only took one break to sit and drink water by his suitcases: next to the neighbor's wooden fence. Ensign's break was cut short, and he jumped backward as a large angry head of a pit bull suddenly appeared at his feet. From underneath the fence, barking and snarling aggressively, the dog seemed angry enough to squeeze through the hole on effort alone. Ensign caught his breath as he put his gun back in his pocket; not even realizing he had pulled it out as he jumped backward in reaction to the dog.

Ensign and the three roofers finished the job as the sky grew dark and the rain began to come down harder. Ensign looked online for a hotel. He couldn't find any vacancies anywhere in that part of Toledo. The roofers assured Ensign they knew a hotel close-by with vacancies. Half an hour later, Ensign hopped from the van in a hotel parking lot.

As two of the guys unloaded Ensign's suitcases for him, the third guy pulled a stack of bills from his pocket. As the third guy, the driver of the van, counted out money; he thanked Ensign for his help finishing the roof. The van pulled away as Ensign walked towards the lobby of the hotel. He had a hundred and fifty dollars in his hand; money he didn't have before he accepted the ride in the windowless van.

Yubikiri

Online, the hotel showed no vacancy. The parking lot was full. People were out and about everywhere. Ensign had a bad feeling as he worked his way to the lobby entrance. He pulled one suitcase and lifted the suitcase with the broken wheel, step by step, as he attempted to get inside the building. Again, Ensign was exhausted and soaked in sweat. The roofing job, though worth it, had taken a lot out of him.

Ensign finally reached the desk in the front lobby, and he rang the bell. As he waited, he collapsed into a seat next to the desk. People were everywhere. Ensign didn't care. With his bags in each of his hands, Ensign closed his eyes to wait for a hotel employee to show up to the desk. Ensign had a bad feeling. The internet showed no vacancy...

"Sir. Sir, may I help you?"

Ensign opened his eyes. "Yeah, please tell me you have a room available."

"No sir, we do not. We are all booked up for the night."

Ensign's heart sank. Just as he took in the words from the Indian guy at the desk, someone else spoke from the other side of the coffee pot in the lobby. It was a younger Mexican guy; clean cut and dressed well. Ensign turned to face him.

"I overheard you can't get a room. I've got a room for the night. I'm waiting to get picked up. You can come hang out in my room while I wait, and then you can stay in it once I leave."

"Dude, thank you so much. That's..."

The hotel clerk cut Ensign off mid-sentence. "There's no shared rooms. It is not allowed."

It took some convincing, but Ensign managed to talk the hotel clerk into allowing him to hang out in the room. He told the clerk he was only going to be there until he found someone to pick him up. It was that, or he would have to sit with his bags in the lobby for the evening. The clerk made the exception, and Ensign walked outside with the young Mexican guy.

That particular hotel had entrance doors to the rooms from the inside hallways and also from outside in the parking lot. The room to which the two of them were headed was halfway down the parking lot. As Ensign walked with his luggage, he took in the scene around him. The hotel was seedy, for sure. Seedy people were out and about everywhere. Ensign didn't care. He was grateful for a place to rest.

Two hours later, the moderate rain began to pick up to a full-on storm. The hotel clerk had been to Derrick's room once earlier to remind Ensign he needed to be out of the room that evening. Once the rain began to fall hard, Ensign knew the clerk wouldn't be by again. Ensign was set for the night. He was concerned, though. Check-out was at eleven o'clock the next morning. Whether Derrick's ride picked him up that night or the next morning, Ensign was still on a timer. Ensign needed to rest, so he put the stress of finding somewhere else to go on the back burner.

Derrick's phone rang. It was his ride. They weren't going to pick him up until check-out the next morning. Derrick was from Toledo, but he just got back from Cincinnati shortly before Ensign was dropped off at the hotel. Derrick had just completed a two-week stint in a rehab facility down in Cincinnati. Derrick, though only nineteen years old, had a half-decade long fentanyl addiction which landed him in some trouble with the law. That two-week period in rehabilitation was the first time he had been clean from the drug since he was fifteen years old.

Derrick stepped out of the room after answering a phone call once it was dark outside. When he returned, Ensign knew Derrick's short-lived sobriety was about to come to an end. Ensign set up his tattoo equipment. Derrick pulled a cigarette cellophane from his pocket and set it on the table. Ensign's mood switched from exhausted to anticipatory. The cellophane on the table was wrapped around twenty little white pills. Ensign didn't need to ask, but he did anyhow. Derrick confirmed that the two of them were about to sniff fentanyl.

Ensign set up his tattoo ink while Derrick used a credit card to smash up some of the pills. The two of them took turns sniffing lines of the powder before Ensign began tattooing. After two lines, Ensign was high. Derrick did three more lines of fentanyl before he sat down in front of Ensign. As Ensign began to tattoo Derrick's wrist, Derrick spoke.

"I have a Narcan nasal spray right here. Just make sure to use it if I overdose."

Ensign finished Derrick's tattoo as Derrick nodded in and out of consciousness. Ensign was high, but he was able to stay awake. After Ensign cleaned up his tattoo equipment, he periodically checked to be sure that Derrick was still breathing. Derrick was seated upright in a chair in the hotel room, his head leaning backward. He was fully unconscious, but his breathing was steady. While Derrick slept, Ensign got on his phone; he needed to figure out what he was going to do when he had to leave the hotel the next morning.

Ensign walked with his two suitcases through Toledo: down Alexis Road. It was noon. The rain from the night before was gone. The sunlight forced Ensign to squint as he walked. He had a half hour. He was a quarter mile from a Taco Bell; one at which he hadn't eaten in years. Ensign wanted to eat before his ride picked him up. He had money from the roofing job. Ensign looked forward to eating at his favorite fast-food restaurant. Though his luggage was weighing him down, with frequent stops to catch his breath, he knew he was going to make it to the restaurant.

An hour earlier, Ensign had solved the problem of where he was going to go once Derrick checked out from the hotel. On a website of classified ads, a particular post stood out amongst the others. The ad, though written to appear innocent and straightforward to the standard viewer, had blatant nefarious undertones to anyone on the level. Ensign, being an astute adult hookup practitioner, noticed the true nature of the online ad. It was perfect, and Ensign knew he had found what he was looking for. Ensign replied to the post. He was soon in a text conversation with a man from a suburb on the other side of the river, south of Toledo.

"M seeking M. Offering room and board for a younger male who is good with his hands. I'm looking for a guy to do handy work and various tasks around my home. I live in a house by myself, and I will provide a private bedroom and meals for a male who fits what I seek. Be young, fit and attractive, 18 to 25. Send picture."

"Hi, I saw your ad. I'm not in your age range. I think if I send you a few pictures, you will make the exception."

"Send pictures."

And like that, Ensign was off and running. He knew what it was that the man in Rossford sought. He also knew he had just done a respectable job down in Texas remodeling Lyla's mobile home. If there were any real work to be done at the house, Ensign had those skills with which to bargain. If not…well, he would cross that bridge when he got to it.

When Derrick checked out of the hotel, Ensign began his walk towards Alexis Road. He was only two blocks south. He knew once he reached that main road that he would be just a short bit from a Taco Bell. Ensign needed to eat. He hadn't eaten in a day. Being off crystal made him less able to ignore his appetite.

Ensign texted with Harrold while he walked, working out the details of the new arrangement. Harrold agreed to meet Ensign at the Taco Bell on Alexis Road that afternoon. Ensign had time to lug his bags from the hotel to the restaurant and get some food. Ensign asked Harrold if he wanted anything to eat. Harrold replied and told Ensign he was on a strict healthy lifestyle diet.

After catching his breath in the Taco Bell parking lot one final time, Ensign headed into the front entrance. He saw no workers inside, on either side of the counter. The restaurant had no other customers inside. The interior walls appeared to be in the process of a paint job. Ensign wondered what was going on, because he had seen cars moving at a normal pace through the drive-through as he walked up to the building. After five minutes, Ensign yelled into the back from the counter.

"Is anyone here? Hello?"

Another minute passed. Finally, a lady in a Taco Bell uniform walked from the back to meet Ensign at the counter.

"Sir, the inside of the restaurant is closed."

"The sign outside says 'open,' and the door was unlocked."

"Well, we're closed. I don't know why the door is unlocked, but it isn't supposed to be."

"Can I get some food? I haven't eaten in a day."

"No sir, you need to leave. The drive through is open."

"Can I walk through the drive through? I don't have a car."

"No sir, you need to be in a car."

Ensign walked out. Coronavirus, though in the past, was still causing problems. Ensign waited for Harrold outside, and he took the time to leave a negative online review for that particular restaurant. After a few more minutes, Harrold pulled up while Ensign sat on the curb. Harrold and Ensign placed

Ensign's two suitcases in the back seats of the car. Ensign hopped in the car, and Harrold took him through the drive thru. While Ensign ate his tacos as he rode in the car, Harrold ate a bag of fruit and nuts which he had brought with him.

The conversation on the way back to Harrold's house centered around expectations. Harrold had his terms; Ensign hoped to change the terms. Harrold told Ensign how his particular dynamics had worked in past situations. Ensign wanted to avoid the bulk of activity which he knew Harrold expected. Ensign was confident that he brought skills to the table in regard to home improvement. If Harrold needed work done at his home, Ensign wanted to shift his role to become the contractor of the home improvement projects.

As Ensign listened to Harrold, he knew his first task was going to be unavoidable. Each time Ensign switched the conversation to the items needed done around the house, Harrold brought it back to his need for a massage. Ensign knew that the massage was going to happen. He prepared himself mentally as the two of them exited the highway by the casino, across the river in Rossford, Ohio. Five minutes later, the car pulled into the driveway. Ensign was ready for his first required task to put the roof over his head; a massage...and whatever else was included with the massage.

Bits and Pieces

Ensign washed the oil from his hands in the upstairs bathroom sink. Down the hallway was Ensign's new bedroom. On the bed, Ensign sorted out the items from his two suitcases. He knew he was going to need Harrold to drive him to his storage unit within the next couple of days. He had items to drop off and other items he wanted to pick up. Ensign sat down on the edge of his new bed, and he thought in silence for a moment. Ensign was lost; his life seemed so unfamiliar. Though he was a mere ten minutes from his old house in Perrysburg, he felt a lifetime away from everything. Whatever he had gotten himself into; it was an improvement from where he was the day before. Ensign had a roof over his head. Harrold was a nice guy…as far as Ensign could tell.

Fortunately, over the next couple of weeks, there were plenty of home improvement projects to keep Ensign busy and earning his keep away from Harrold's bedroom. That massage on the first day was the only time Ensign had to bend to the agreement which was implied in the online classified ad. Harrold had many home projects, and Ensign had the skills needed to put in the work. Digging up a cement fire pit, moving and leveling a shed, creating a rock garden, redoing the glassed-in front porch, painting and tiling the kitchen wall and floor, any other random item which came up; Ensign stayed busy while he lived with Harrold in Rossford.

Ensign went above and beyond. Harrold saw the work and paid Ensign cash on top of room and board. Harrold farmed Ensign out to his mother. Harrold's mother lived across the city, and Harrold dropped Ensign off at her house for three full workdays. At the end of those three days, Ensign had removed two large trees from her yard and cleared out the overgrowth around the garage in the backyard. Harrold's mom was pleased with Ensign's work. She paid seven hundred dollars for Ensign's effort. With that, and the money Harrold paid to Ensign for work on his house, Ensign had over a grand which he didn't have before.

Ensign was at a pivotal point. Though he hadn't done crystal in a while, he knew he wanted to get back in the scene. Ensign knew he finally had enough money to buy a quantity worth buying. Though Ensign was no longer in contact with his sources, he knew someone who could put him on. Since he first met Meg on the website, back when he was staying in Michigan and building his Subaru camper/car, Meg always had substantial amounts of crystal from a source independent of Ensign. Ensign remained in touch with Meg through all his tribulations and travel during 2021. Meg wanted to see Ensign again if he ever returned to the Midwest. Ensign knew it was time to let Meg know that he was back...and that he was looking to party.

Ensign was feeling good. From betting ten dollars on a slot machine, he was up a hundred and twenty. Ensign knew his luck wouldn't last, so he walked outside to wait for Meg to arrive. Meg pulled up to Ensign as he stood in the parking garage of the casino. Ensign hopped in her car. The two of them hugged. It had been almost a year since Meg and Ensign last saw each other. Meg was still as pretty as Ensign remembered.

"So where are we headed?"

"Well, my guy won't be around for a few more hours. I have a place by my house I want to take you."

McCourtie Park, in Somerset Center, Michigan, was a wonderful experience. Ensign held hands with Meg as she showed him around. The seventeen bridges, wooden in appearance, were all actually cement sculptures. The bridges, sculpted by Mexican immigrant expert cement artists George Cardoso and Ralph Corona in the 1930s, spanned the various creeks and waterways which meandered through the park. Meg shared the history of the place, having grown up and lived a stone's throw away. There were mafia connections and rumors of underground passages. There were rumors of bodies entombed beneath the cement structures on the grounds.

Ensign took in the sights and the moments with Meg. He expressed his appreciation for her and for her sharing the experience with him. Though Ensign's year was not going anything like he had hoped, his time that day with Meg was a welcome reprieve. With the flowers of the botanical gardens as a backdrop, Ensign and Meg shared a kiss which took Ensign away from all the negativity he had experienced in 2021. For that afternoon, Ensign forgot about everything which wasn't that moment in time. For that afternoon, Ensign was happy. In that moment, life was again amazing.

As Meg and Ensign explored the park together, they took note of the various groups of well-dressed high school aged kids walking around and posing for pictures together. The kids were dressed formally, dresses and tuxedos. Ensign remembered being that age; his whole life ahead of him. He smiled at the thought. He gazed at Meg. She seemed to be deep in thought as well; maybe thinking the same thing. Meg's phone rang. It was her guy. They had to go. The afternoon at the park was done.

Ensign sat in a bedroom with a twitchy guy. Ensign and the guy conversed while they passed a mirror back and forth to do hotrails. Meg and another guy had left the house to make a run to score drugs. The twitchy guy was sharing his personal supply of crystal with Ensign as they waited for the two others to return. Ensign was high again. It had been a minute. He was content. He knew he was again going to have a large quantity of crystal to get him through.

It was raining hard later that night when Meg and Ensign

arrived at Meg's parents' house in Hillsdale, Michigan. The house was huge. It was divided into two sections, connected by a section of hallways in the middle. The rain was flooding the grounds of the farm property outside the house. Meg found a place to park amongst the mud and puddles. The two of them ran through the rain and dark to reach the section of the house where Meg was living. Though Meg told Ensign to be quiet once they got inside, Ensign wasn't too worried about waking Meg's parents; they were fast asleep and far away, upstairs in the other section of the house.

Once inside, Ensign cooked food. The two of them took off their wet clothes and ate before they went upstairs to do drugs in Meg's section of the home. Though Ensign and Meg kissed throughout the night as they did methamphetamine, they never took it any farther. Meg painted pictures while Ensign explored the large room. Both of them ended up falling asleep in an entertainment room, amongst storage items and below the vaulted ceiling. Ensign had two ounces of crystal, enough to keep him high for a long time. He slept well that night at Meg's house.

The next morning, the house was alive with people. Ensign met Meg's parents. He also met her sister, her brothers, and their children, all of whom had stopped over to the house for a cookout. After eating, Meg took Ensign back from Michigan to Harrold's house in Rossford, Ohio. Ensign thanked Meg for her help scoring the drugs. In his goodbye to her, as they hugged and kissed, Ensign told Meg he looked forward to seeing her again in the near future.

Redacted

Ensign, as with previous dynamics, knew his time at Harrold's house was coming to an end. He finished all the home improvement projects. He wasn't paying for his room and board with any sexual favors. He saw that Harrold felt it was getting to be time they parted ways. Though he ate meals with Harrold, and sometimes some of Harrold's friends who came over for dinner, Ensign mainly kept to himself at all other times. Ensign worked out with Harrold's weights in the basement. He wore the clothes Harrold had given him. He interacted online from his bedroom, and Alyssa, Jane's doppelganger, picked him up on occasion to get high at her house. Alyssa dropped Ensign off one afternoon. When Ensign walked inside, Harrold began the conversation which Ensign had been expecting.

"So, it looks like all the work around here is done."

"Unless you have anything else…"

"Do you think you can find a place to go by the end of the week?"

"I'll do what I can. I should be able to. Harrold, thank you for the hospitality."

"Well, thank you for the hard work you did around here. I'm grateful for it. I hope staying here helped you out."

"It did, for sure. I really appreciate it. I'll work on getting out of here."

When the next week began, Harrold helped Ensign load his

belongings into the car. Ensign hadn't found a place to go, but he knew he wasn't able to stay at Harrold's house any longer. As Harrold dropped Ensign off at his storage unit, Ensign assured Harrold he would figure something out from there.

"Are you sure you'll be alright from here."

"No worries, man. I'll get it sorted. Again, thank you for having me and paying me for working."

"Thank you. You did a great job."

"Well, who knows what the future holds. We were meant to cross paths. Maybe we will again down the road."

"Take care."

Ensign watched Harrold's car pull out of the storage complex and disappear into the morning. As Ensign unlocked his storage unit, he truly didn't know what he was going to do. He was alone with all he owned in the entire world. He was at a storage unit outside of Perrysburg, Ohio; the city where he grew up and spent most of his life.

Ensign's storage unit was facing out of the complex. Across the auxiliary road on the other side of the fence were the township softball diamonds. At the far end of the complex, the auxiliary road ended at two factories. Down the other end of the road, past the building where the offices to the storage company were housed, was the entrance to the main road which ran two miles down to Perrysburg. On the backside of the particular building which housed his unit, there were four other rows of storage unit buildings which ran parallel to his particular unit, all the way down to the factories at the end of the road.

Ensign's unit was only six units deep on the front side, facing the auxiliary road and softball diamonds. Dozens of other units lined the building, and the next building down from him, all the way to the fence dividing the complex from the factories at the end of the road. Along the fences on the far side and opposite side of the complex, boats and vehicles were parked for storage.

It was late summer, almost the beginning of fall. It was hot outside, both day and night. The heat from inside the metal storage unit hit Ensign as he opened the roll-up door to place his items inside. Harrold was gone. The softball diamonds were empty. It was still too early in the year for softball season. Ensign hadn't seen anyone at the storage complex when he punched in the gate code and Harrold drove him to his unit inside the complex.

The Sun was shining brightly that morning. Birds were randomly chirping from locations close by. As Ensign stood on the pavement in front of his open storage unit, he gazed past the fence which lined the outside of the paved ground of the complex. He was alone, a million miles away from where he grew up; just down the street.

In the moment, Ensign's mind was elsewhere. His storage unit, loaded up with furniture, weights, and everything he had accumulated in a lifetime on Earth, was filled from top to bottom, front to back. There was a small area of cement floor, three feet by three feet, in the front of the unit. The floor space was void of Ensign's belongings. Ensign climbed up on a stack of his belongings and retrieved a folding chair.

He opened the chair and placed it in the small open spot on the pavement. Despite the heat, Ensign rolled down the metal door to his unit with him inside. The light inside the unit, coming in from gaps above, was enough to see what he was doing. Sweat poured from Ensign as he sat down on the folding chair, surrounded by his belongings in his closed-up storage unit. Ensign removed his drug equipment and his bag of crystal from his backpack. As he sat alone, pouring sweat in the almost dark storage unit, while amongst everything he had collected in a lifetime no longer seeming his own, Ensign blew down hotrails for the next hour without break.

Ensign had seen so many high points on his journey through the country, and his own mind since the adventure began in

2018. Ensign had made it through many low points as well; the bulk of them taking place in the most recent year. He had gained lifetimes of experience, and he had felt lifetimes worth of emotions. Ensign had lived like he never knew was possible. He had suffered like he never knew was possible. He'd met so many people and shared so many unique interactions. He'd seen more than he could have ever imagined. He'd lost more than he knew he had to lose.

As Ensign sat there in his storage unit, outside of his home city where it all began, he couldn't wrap his mind around all which had become his life since he made that initial deal with himself just three years earlier, in his previous home just a couple of miles from where he sat. Life had been good. Ensign felt like he had truly lived. He knew how amazing his experience had been. As Ensign sat and thought of so many different things, he failed to think of what was to come. There was no way he could have had the thought because he hadn't yet lived the experience. That experience began that day as he sat there and smoked meth in his rented storage unit. Ensign began a journey that sunny morning in late summer of 2021. Ensign wasn't ready for it, but he had no choice. It was time, and he would have to live it.

Ensign was forty-one years old. Forty-one years of experiences, good, bad, and everything in between. Forty-one years of making it through tough times and situations, balanced out with high points and personal growth. In those forty-one years, Ensign managed to keep going. A lifetime of change and perseverance, through everything life threw at him, led him to where he was.

2021 had been a series of incremental challenges to Ensign, each predicament somehow lower than the situation before it. Ensign kept wondering what else could go wrong. He had made it through each decline in living, just to be faced with a harder challenge. He learned he was strong enough to continue, but he wasn't sure he wanted to continue. Ensign didn't know it as he sat in that folding chair, but he was about to experience life to the actual worst degree. His number was up, and his time had come. Everything led him to that sunny morning in Ohio; the morning which marked the beginning of a nightmare at Ensign's true rock bottom.

There's No Place Like Home

That first night was a mental journey through negativity. As the Sun went down, a storm swept in. It seemed fitting. A storm was raging in Ensign's mind, as well. With the metal roller-door fully shut, and a screwdriver jammed in the side rail to effectively lock the door, Ensign frantically sorted through his belongings. He hurried to move whatever he could away from the base of the door. Water from the severe thunderstorm began to wash underneath the metal and onto the cement floor.

The hard rain's relentless pounding on the metal storage structure was deafening. Once Ensign climbed over some couches, with a flashlight in his mouth, he found some old ear plugs in a drawer of a dresser. Up high in the towers of storage, the smaller dresser was stacked closer to the ceiling, on top of another dresser. Ensign put in the ear plugs. With the plugs blocking out most of the noise from the rain, Ensign's thoughts seemed only louder.

The remnants of a life lost, stacked and packed all around him. Floor to ceiling high, front to back; everything Ensign had accumulated and held onto from the beginning of his existence. Boxes of family picture albums, the baby book his mom began keeping at the end of 1979, stacks of totes containing what was left of Ensign's childhood; action figures, games, figurines, everything in the entire world which still belonged to Ensign.

There were appliances and furniture, there were collections of books, music, and movies. In every available gap between tables and gym equipment, there was box after box, each filled with random items such as electronics and dishes. Car parts were strewn about on stacks of other items. There was a living room set in the front. There was a disassembled queen-sized bed in the back corner. An old, floor-model projection television held two wall-sized mirrors against the side of the metal storage unit. A washing machine in the back corner was stuffed full of fake plants from Ensign's old office. The matching dryer, long gone; given to his friend Jane back when he rented a room from her long ago.

Ensign was there inside the metal box, amongst four decades of everything. Ensign had time, he had treasures to uncover and sort, and he had enough crystal to fuel the exploratory mission for the unforeseeable future. That was it; Ensign's mind was breaking down and his distraction was his tomb; he was relegated to reside amongst ghosts and memories of a life no longer his own.

Ensign was entombed with all he possessed in the world, but he was still breathing as he lay alone on piles of his own history. There was so much there with him in the contained chaos and disorganization of what once made sense. All of it meant nothing and was nothing; distractions and tasks to occupy time as the crystal dictated, how the crystal dictated. Ensign floated there in suspended animation; reunited with his past belongings in petrified time and space.

Ensign was in Hell; he was living his rock bottom. It was a realization which was blatant and obvious from that stormy first night. He no longer wondered when his luck was going to turn around. He no longer wondered what else was going to go wrong. He knew he was in it.

His mind broke as he poured sweat, locked in his metal box of everything which he spent the previous years trying to escape. His mind, his Hell. His storage unit; a reminder of the mess inside his brain. A reminder which had become his entire world; all which was in his immediate presence, surrounding him at every moment of every day and night. It was no longer a storage unit of Ensign's belongings; it was Ensign's entire world. There was no line where the inner turmoil ended, and the outside clutter began. Ensign's mind, and his world around him; it was all one big mess.

Basic Necessities

Shelter: There was no electricity and no running water in Ensign's metal box. There was no bathroom or kitchen. The heat from the Sun; it mixed with the lack of air circulation and kept Ensign in a perpetual sauna. On the weekends, when the office and groundskeeping staff were away, Ensign could roll up the garage door for airflow. For the first week, Ensign could keep the door open in the evenings once staff went home for the day. Softball season began only a week after Ensign moved into the storage unit. Softball was played most nights for a couple of hours, and many times, on the weekends. Since Ensign's storage unit directly faced the softball diamond and bleachers, Ensign had to keep the large roll-up door shut until games ended. That meant the Sun, from sunup to sundown, cooked Ensign inside the stuffy metal box.

Food and drinks: There was nowhere within two miles for Ensign to acquire meals and hydration. Fortunately, Ensign's friend Lex frequently sent him money to order food from a delivery service. On the days when Ensign sweated out all of his hydration, nothing was better than seeing the delivery driver pull up to the gate of the complex. Ensign had to wait to order food and drinks until the storage unit staff went home each night. Without refrigeration, Ensign needed to be sure not to overorder. His garbage was walked across the road to a garbage can at the softball diamond in the middle of the night. There were days when Ensign had no hydration remaining in him from cooking in the Sun and sorting through his storage items, and the delivery drivers would forget the drinks. Those days were a challenge; both physically and mentally.

Mental Challenges

Paranoia: During the hours from early morning until evening, Ensign remained completely silent inside his metal box. The grounds crew for the complex was always about. Workers from the office passed by his unit. Others with storage units frequently visited their units. Ensign could hear everything from all the people at the complex. He remained silent for many hours on end each day to avoid detection. The crystal, the heat, and the lack of sleep took their toll on Ensign's fried brain. He heard voices discussing how it was known that he was living in the storage unit. Ensign would then climb to the top of his belongings on the side of the roll-up door to peek out from the top by the roller, only to see nobody anywhere near the front of his unit. Since he never knew what was real, he remained silent at almost all times.

Mindset: The isolation and physical discomfort took a quick toll on Ensign's chemically cooked brain. Depression was at the forefront; Ensign immersed himself in sorting through his belongings in silence while closed inside his nightmare box. With a flashlight, Ensign sorted out belongings which he figured he could find ways to sell and make money to keep eating and drinking. The crystal propelled Ensign to new levels of obsession and compulsion while surrounded by memories of his no-longer life. Though the drugs kept Ensign going, they also hyper-emphasized any bad thoughts which floated into Ensign's brain. Everything surrounding Ensign reminded him of various parts of his past. He was immersed in triggers for thoughts he didn't want to think.

The Scene

There was so much packed into such a small area around Ensign. As the clouds of crystal smoke dissipated through the cracks of the metal ceiling grating and into the adjacent units, Ensign poured sweat while frantically sorting through remnants of his former life. Full days were spent on individual missions to locate and organize. Other days were spent shifting ceiling-high stacks of his belongings to try to create new places to rest. Countless boxes were emptied and reloaded with other items. Each attempt to organize left more of a mess than before. The pile of belongings appeared to have been bulldozed into the unit. Floor to ceiling, all the way from the door to the back wall, the enclosed disaster consumed Ensign physically and mentally.

There was a day when Ensign figured he couldn't make progress because there was nowhere to move anything to begin any real organization. Ensign began at six o'clock in the morning. By midday, seventy-five percent of Ensign's hoard was on the pavement outside his unit. From two units down, on either side, and all the way to the fence on the side of the storage complex, Ensign's belongings filled the ground. That disaster caught the attention of the front office. Ensign was visited by employees at three separate times that morning.

At noon, the owner of the complex drove up to the outside of the fence on the auxiliary road, between the complex and the softball diamond. The complex owner jumped from his pickup truck and angrily walked over to the fence. After some choice words, he hopped back in his truck and sped off. Ensign agreed to have the mess cleaned up by the end of the day, but he knew that meant he was going to be working well into the night. He planned to do that anyhow. He had nowhere to go, and crystal was fueling his actions.

It ended up taking until three o'clock the following morning for Ensign to use a snow shovel to finally shovel the last of his belongings off the pavement outside. All the broken items and garbage with nowhere else to go were loaded back into the storage unit, along with the items Ensign sorted out over that entire day. The wall of debris was barely contained when Ensign tried to roll down the overhead door. It took another hour of attempting to push the pile back away from the track of the door at the front of the unit before he was finally able to close himself and his belongings inside to remain for the rest of the work week. That morning, Ensign slept for a few hours, three quarters of the way up the side of a stack of his belongings.

"Imagine loading all your belongings from your entire house and garage into a large semi-trailer. Then imagine the trailer being turned up on its end and everything dumped out into a pile; some items break, some boxes break open, nothing in any semblance of order. Imagine then living there with the mess, enclosed in four metal walls and a metal roof, creating garbage daily from biproducts of life…in extreme heat, and with no bathroom, barely able to fit."

Ensign sent the text to Lex, and he included a picture from his current vantage point where he sat, in the passenger seat from his old BMW; on top of a dresser which was balanced on a table, with boxes and debris piled up to that top layer of hoard. Ensign turned to reach up to remove a drawer from a nightstand above him, to his right. As he pulled out the drawer, the weight from the contents caused it to slide out quicker than Ensign was able to react.

The corner of the drawer hit Ensign and split the bridge of his nose. Everything from inside the drawer fell around Ensign and tumbled down the piles of hoard. Ensign, seeing stars, fell backward down the pile where he had been perched. Luckily, he managed to grab onto some gym equipment as he fell. He carefully slid the rest of the way to a stop on top of a stack of boxes. He reached his hand to his face. Blood steadily trickled from Ensign's face, and drops of blood rained down to the hoard below.

When one of the wall-length mirrors shattered, there were suddenly shards of glass to contend with; mixed in amongst the hoard which was Ensign's life. A glass end table broke one day when Ensign was climbing to the back of the pile; more glass to manage on the excursions of discovery. Especially in the dark, Ensign was prone to catching a glass shard in a hand or a leg. The terrain was treacherous, but the treasures found were worth the injuries.

Alyssa, Jane's doppelganger, stopped by Ensign's new home on various occasions. Ensign let go of a little crystal each time she stopped by, and Alyssa helped fund the storage life. Alyssa met Ensign at the gate, Ensign punched in the code, the gate opened, and Alyssa drove around to Ensign's unit. The two of them, barely able to fit amongst the clutter of Ensign's hoard, closed themselves into storage and blew down hotrails inside the metal box.

One day, after Ensign went on an exploratory mission, Alyssa called Ensign's phone. She was looking to score a small amount of crystal, and Ensign needed a ride. It was a fair trade. Ensign got Alyssa high, and Alyssa took Ensign to a comic book shop across town. Ensign had searched, and he found his tote full of action figures from his childhood. Ensign parted ways with his action figures that day. A childhood of memories, sold for enough money to get him through the next week.

There was no electricity in Ensign's unit, but he had a solution. In the evenings, after the office workers went home for the day, Ensign took walks. He walked to the end of the building. Around the corner, on the short side of the building, there were electrical outlets. Ensign had multiple extension cords, forty feet long and twenty feet long. After connecting six of the cords, he was able to reach his unit from the power outlets.

Ensign plugged in a box fan, a lamp, and a power strip to the end of the cords inside of his unit. He was able to charge his phone in the middle of the night. He had light to see what he was perpetually sorting, and the breeze from the fan was a relief from the hot and stale air of the metal box. Each morning, at five o'clock, Ensign made sure to unplug and wind up his cords so when the staff arrived for the day, they were none the wiser.

There were many things which were only able to be done in the middle of the night when nobody else was anywhere close. The streetlamps at the far end of the complex, all the way down by the factories at the end of the road; underneath those was the only place bright enough to manage certain tasks. Ensign took two broken pieces of the wall mirror and his electric shaver to that far end of the complex. In the middle of the night, Ensign used those items to line himself up. Homemade haircuts took place at three in the morning.

In the middle of the night, Ensign was far into a journey inside his metal box. He was up high, close to the roller door, on a precarious stack of his belongings. Items shifted beneath his feet. Ensign struggled for stability, and he hopped up another level closer to the top. A heavy glass coffee table shifted below him. Suddenly, the coffee table fell. The table caught on the closed roller door. Seconds later, an avalanche cascaded down the pile to rest on top of the coffee table. The weight was too much, and the roller door broke free from the metal which fastened it to the top of the unit.

The door, and the roller on the side of the unit; it all dropped from up by the ceiling. Ensign and his hoard were instantly exposed. As he stared out to the night sky beyond the storage building, Ensign's heart began to race. Not only had he just broken the roller door, but he had exposed everything to the outside world. The door was still hanging from the other side, but there was a gap of emptiness from the ceiling to the ground.

Ensign and his hoard were exposed to the world.

It ended up taking eight hours. Eight hours after the door fell, Ensign secured it back in position. Ensign could barely catch his breath. He was physically exhausted. He sacrificed two belts and three ratchet straps, but he fixed it. Standing high up against the ceiling of the storage unit, Ensign managed to tie off the heavy metal roller door. It still functioned, and it again shielded Ensign from the outside world. Straps and belts were tied from the top of the door to various metal beams along the corner of the ceiling. The roller was then bolted back into place. He had done it, and just in time. Moments later, the staff began to arrive at the facility for their morning work shifts.

Some evenings and nights, Ensign ventured out. It was two miles down the main road to reach the shopping strips on the outskirts of Perrysburg proper. Ensign prepared for each journey. With his headphones and phone charged, he strapped his gun to his ankle for the walk. At night, he carried a flashlight. The walks were arduous, but they were breaks from the monotony of being alone and closed-up in a metal cube.

Some days, Ensign made trips to eat at his favorite Greek restaurant. Only one pizza place delivered all the way out to Ensign's storage unit, so he was perpetually sick of it. The walks to the Greek restaurant were a welcomed change. Walmart and Meijer were two miles away. Certain toiletries were needed, as imagined. Ensign wore a backpack on those trips. It made it easier to carry purchased items the two miles back down the road. Ensign felt he accomplished something on those days when he made the four-mile round trip.

Some days, the storms rolled in. Northwest Ohio, in the Midwest, was prone to severe weather. Ensign loved storms, even when he was immediately facing the elements. If he had his belongings strewn about outside his storage unit while sorting them through, he kept an eye out for clouds rolling in. Sometimes, Lex would text him warnings of impending extreme weather.

Ensign then did all he could to re-load his belongings back into storage before the rain and wind hit. Sometimes, he made it; all his items and he closed up in his metal box to wait out the weather. Other times, Ensign got soaked as he finished loading his sopping wet treasures into his home, hoping he managed to get any water-soluble belongings away from the threat.

The lightning in the distance was always beautiful. A sign of immediate peril. The dark clouds on the horizon gave Ensign a feeling of excitement. As the sky grew black, the wind picked up, and the ominous feeling of what was to come was blatant. Ensign prepared himself to wait it out. He knew when to move things off of the inside ground near the roller door, and he knew when he was about to be closed in for the duration. There was a peacefulness amongst the weather's chaos. Ensign knew he was alone, for sure, for the duration of any extreme storm which swept through.

Ensign was always on alert. The factories at the end of the auxiliary road seemed to operate around the clock. Ensign watched, through binoculars, the workers take breaks incrementally around the clock. He did his best to go unnoticed. He did his best to not exist. On occasions, police cruisers patrolled down the auxiliary road, from the main road, past storage and the softball diamond, to the far end of industry. If Ensign was outside, he acted nonchalant. If he was in his unit with the door cracked for ventilation, he closed the door completely and dealt with the stale air until the police were gone.

One night, at one o'clock in the morning, Ensign was caught off guard. His crystal-fueled brain was too preoccupied as he sorted out car speaker components. As he stood, just inside the threshold of storage, a police officer was suddenly standing right behind him. Ensign wasn't ready for the interaction. He instantly covered his drug paraphernalia as the officer made his presence known.

"Hi, sir. We got a call of some activity here tonight…"

"Well, yeah. I guarantee you it was my activity."

"What are you…wait a minute. I remember you. Last month…"

"Yes. Wow, that was you, wasn't it?"

"You told me your story; how you're sorting your storage unit. Well, you sure are. Still going, huh?"

Fortune was in Ensign's favor that night. That same officer, the one who was so cool despite Ensign having a handgun on his ankle and pulling his luggage through a parking lot a mile away. It was the same officer. Ensign had rapport, and he was put at ease from the familiar face. The two of them conversed for the next ten minutes. Ensign was actually happy to have some company. After some parting words, the officer left Ensign to his project. Ensign shook his head. He was amazed that he saw that same officer again.

There were days when direct storage neighbors spent time at their units. It was usually on Sundays. Once in a while, both next door neighbors showed up at the same time. Ensign was effectively surrounded on those days. He did what he could to blend in, just another guy, randomly at his storage unit. Some days, Ensign was closed inside when his neighbors arrived. He remained silent until they left, whether it was minutes or hours.

Other times, there wasn't any way to avoid being seen. Ensign did all he could to appear to be going about normal activities at his unit. He interacted with his neighbors, typical greetings and small talk. Ensign worked while the neighbors pulled out their jet-skis and hooked them to their trucks. Ensign acted busy when his neighbors stopped by to load items into their storage.

From All the Slippin'

It was dark in the unit. The sunlight coming in from the gaps, up by the front of the ceiling where it met the roller, was enough to see. The heat was almost unbearable when Ensign woke up. Though he continuously wiped away the sweat with a towel, he couldn't keep up. Ensign touched the inside of the metal rollup door. He pulled his hand back instantly in reaction to the burn. Ensign wiped sweat from his body one more time, and he began gathering up items from the cramped space around him.

Within an hour, Ensign had two bags packed. Tattoo equipment, drug paraphernalia, and adult novelty items filled his backpack. His suitcase was filled with clothes and toiletries, enough to cover the three days he was about to spend in a hotel. Ensign also had a stack of totes and boxes separated out from the rest of his hoard. The containers were filled with all of Ensign's books, his DVDs and Blue rays, his video games and multiple game consoles, and a couple of old laptops. Ensign's entire collections of his media; all he had carefully curated over four decades, nine large boxes and totes, hundreds of pounds from a lifetime of collection, everything was stacked there in the front corner of the storage unit.

Over the previous week, Ensign was in contact with a friend of his from Toledo. His friend had recently opened a store in the city. The store was a second-hand video and bookstore. Ensign knew what he had to do. Though he wished he could avoid it, Ensign needed the money and the extra space in his storage unit. Ensign's friend was expecting him in the upcoming week. Ensign was going to sell his complete collection. Over the prior week, Ensign spent hours locating, sorting, and packing all of it into those nine totes and boxes. His opportunity to transport his belongings was coming.

Ensign met Shannon at the gate to the storage complex. He punched in the gate code, and Shannon drove around to the front of Ensign's storage unit. Shannon was in town from Florida for four days. She had business obligations and family to see. Ensign was about to get a reprieve from the storage unit. He hadn't showered in weeks, he hadn't had air conditioning, and he hadn't slept in a bed. Ensign was overdue for all of it.

After Shannon helped Ensign load his media into the trunk and back seats of her rental car, Ensign grabbed his two bags and hopped in the passenger seat. The air conditioning was instantly amazing. Shannon had a stop to make before she checked into her hotel. Shannon's mom's house was down the road, in Perrysburg. Shannon's mom was out of town, but Shannon needed to stop by and pick up some mail which was there for her.

Ensign showered as Shannon sat in the bathroom and sorted through her mail. It was a luxury in which Ensign hadn't realized he had been missing as much as he had. While in the shower, Ensign blew down hotrails. Shannon walked over to him after each one. Ensign kissed the smoke from his lungs into Shannon's mouth. By the end of the shower, Shannon was higher than she had been since Ensign last saw her in Florida in spring.

Once Shannon checked into the hotel in Rossford, the two of them continued their dynamic up in the hotel room. Ensign remained unclothed, and in the room, for the duration. When Shannon left for work and family obligations, Ensign used the time to tattoo himself, make videos for her, and craft new adult toys with hot glue sticks and a blowtorch. Ensign stayed high the entire time, same as he had been doing in his storage unit. When Shannon returned from each excursion, Ensign quickly got her high again, and the two of them put Ensign's newly created adult novelty items to work together.

On their last day together, Shannon drove Ensign to his

friend's store in Toledo. Ensign used a hand cart to lug all of his boxes and totes from Shannon's car into the store. After a few moments of catching up with his friend, Ensign left his lifetime of media items at the store in Toledo. He left with no money because all of his items needed to be sorted and priced. Ensign was told to expect payment by the end of the week. It was a lot to sort out, and Ensign understood it was going to take some time.

Ensign wasn't happy when he left the store. He felt a sadness of loss. He felt as if he had just parted with a huge component of a long-lost life; now even further removed from his current situation. Those items, especially his book collection, represented a simpler time, a more innocent and carefree part of a previous life. Ensign told Shannon of the hole he felt as they drove back to Perrysburg. Shannon said she understood, but Ensign doubted she actually knew.

Unloading media items sparked a new crystal-fueled obsession in Ensign's cooked brain: clearing out space in the storage unit. Though Ensign sold off much of his gym equipment back when he left his house at the end of 2018, he still had many more fitness items in storage. He had two benches, a squat rack, a universal gym with every attachment, Olympic bars, dumbbells, Olympic plates, a weight tree, a dumbbell rack, and a leg-press machine. A lot of space was occupied by equipment which was not getting used. Ensign posted an ad online. He knew his equipment was going to sell fast, especially at the price point he set in the ad.

Within minutes, Ensign began fielding responses to his post. A man in Michigan told Ensign he would be there at six in the morning with a trailer and the money for the gym equipment. Ensign told the guy to call him when he arrived the next morning, and he closed out of the app. Ensign had been awake for a couple of days at that point, so he spent the rest of the day smoking crystal inside his storage unit. His goal was to stay awake so he could meet the guy the next morning at six o'clock. Ensign did a last hotrail at four in the morning. His body carried him no further. Ensign fell asleep on a fold-out loveseat amongst his gym equipment and all of his other possessions.

At ten o'clock the next morning, Ensign woke up with a jolt. He saw the light coming in around the gap between the roller door and the ceiling. As when he used to sleep through his alarm and see his room lit up on days when he should have been at work well before the Sun came up, Ensign knew he missed the six o'clock transaction with the guy from Michigan. He quickly did a hotrail, and he checked his phone. Sure enough, he missed calls from the guy. Ensign sent an apology message, and he assured the guy he was there and able to sell his equipment. It was too late. The guy was back up in Michigan, unable to make a return trip.

Ensign opened the app where his ad was still posted. He replied to the next message. An hour later, a man and his wife pulled into the complex in a pickup truck which was pulling a flatbed trailer. After another hour, Ensign located the last dumbbell amongst the hoard in the storage unit. The benches and universal gym had been strapped down to the trailer. The dumbbell and plates had been loaded into the back of the pickup truck. Ensign ironically got in a last pump from the workout caused by loading up all of the gym equipment which he no longer owned.

Before the couple left the complex, Ensign asked them if they saw anything else they wanted from his storage unit. The wife bought a few of Ensign's fake plants. She wanted them to decorate her office. The couple also caught sight of something else. The cornhole boards were leaning up against an entertainment center. The boards, made by Ensign's dad as a birthday gift, each had the prism from the cover of Pink Floyd's Dark Side of the Moon album painted across the tops of them. Those boards had been used many times at the house which Ensign once lived in with his wife. Those boards carried memories of a life which didn't even seem real to Ensign anymore. Ensign named a price, and the couple agreed to it. As the couple drove away, Ensign felt that same hollow feeling which he felt when he parted with his books and movies. Ensign was dismantling his former life, pieces at a time.

Take It Down, Pass It Around

The days were still uncomfortably hot, but Ensign felt the seasons beginning to change. As autumn approached, the nights grew cold. Though it was a relief from the incessant heat, the cold nights became a new concern; one which Ensign knew he would eventually have to face. Though his goal, since beginning his life of travel, was always to be down South during the cold Midwest winters, Ensign somehow never managed to completely avoid the winter seasons. As the nights began to get cold. Ensign remained in his storage unit. He knew he wasn't going to survive a winter in northwest Ohio without a car or electricity while inside the metal box. Each cold night was a reminder that his situation was temporary, one way or another.

As was Ensign's luck, his phone broke as he sat inside his storage unit and sorted out some of his belongings. The phone was Ensign's lifeline; it was how he interacted with others, it was how he ordered food and drinks. Ensign's situation instantly went from bad to worse. Fortunately, he received a delivery from an online grocery app the night before. He had wet wipes and paper towels; he had two gallons of water and canned food. Ensign wasn't in immediate peril in that moment when his phone no longer functioned, but he knew he was going to need to take a journey on foot a couple of miles into the city very soon.

Ensign decided he was going to take that walk later on that day once the hot Sun began to go down. The rest of the day was spent smoking crystal and attending to the perpetual need to sort out and organize the hoard inside his storage unit. He had open space after selling his gym equipment. His stacks, piles, bags, and boxes still extended from floor to ceiling, but Ensign managed to uncover some floor space down the very center of the unit. Everything was packed tightly on both sides of the space, from the side walls to the gap in the middle. There was a five-foot-wide walkway of clear floor from the front to the back between the towers of items.

The fold-out loveseat fit there in the gap, which gave Ensign a comfortable place to sleep. The gap was comfortable real estate which allowed Ensign to move, and it allowed Ensign to temporarily move items into the open space to re-sort and organize. Though Ensign had been at the task of reorganization around the clock during the whole time he resided in the metal box, he was nowhere close to any semblance of neat and organized. The bags of garbage he produced, just from living confined in his storage unit, only added to the perpetual disorganization. His job, fueled by drugs, would never be complete.

Caught up in the task at hand, Ensign worked too late into the evening. The Sun went down, and he hadn't even noticed; distracted while moving, sorting, and re-stacking as much as he could. As he finally sat down for a moment's reprieve, Ensign realized he needed to begin walking. He had miles to cover, and he was pushing it with time constraints. Ever since the pandemic, the stores which used to remain open twenty-four hours no longer operated a third shift. Ensign's two options, Meijer and Walmart, both closed at eleven o'clock each night. Though it was late, Ensign figured he could still make it in time.

As he walked in the dark down the state highway to Perrysburg, Ensign did all he could to brush off the mosquitos and not trip on the uneven ground on the side of the road. When cars approached and passed him by at highway speeds, Ensign made sure to shine his flashlight down onto himself to avoid being unseen and potentially run over. Ensign had his backpack on. Inside of it, his broken phone and another shirt; a shirt into which to change when he reached the store. He knew he was going to be completely soaked in sweat from the walk. He was already soaked through his sleeveless shirt from spending the day sorting items in his hot metal box. Ensign had on shorts, which was a mistake due to the mosquitos in the air. He wore his red Air Force Ones on his feet. His feet ached from the walk. Ensign also had his handgun strapped in plain view on his ankle.

When Ensign reached the parking lots of the stores and strip malls, he saw that he had, most-likely, miscalculated. His timing was off. Without a working phone, he didn't know the exact time. He realized the approximate time as he saw the last cars pull out from the parking lots. Ensign still crossed the parking lot to reach the front of the store, but he already knew what was about to happen. Nothing, nothing happened when he stepped in front of the doors. They didn't open. Meijer was closed.

Ensign walked down the pavement in front of the strip malls. He crossed a side street and walked past the stores of the next strip mall. Ensign knew Walmart was also going to be closed, but he checked anyhow. Again, nothing happened when he stood in front of the doors to Walmart. Ensign shook his head and walked across the parking lot to the gas station in the middle of the sea of blacktop. Ensign approached the window. A clerk walked up to talk to him on the intercom from behind the glass, inside the convenience store. Ensign had one question.

"Hi. Do you happen to know what time it is?"

"Yeah, it's eleven fifteen."

Ensign walked around to the other side of the building. He stepped behind a bush near the back wall. Shielded from the spotlights of the parking lot, Ensign unzipped and relieved himself in the dark. He couldn't hold it in any longer, and outdoors was his only option. There was a picnic table close to the gas station, on a small island of grass in the parking lot. Ensign sat down. He sprayed himself with bug spray from his backpack. He was hot and exhausted. He didn't want to walk the two miles in the dark; just to need to make another trip to the store the next morning. Ensign sat, and he thought of options while he rested from the walk.

Ensign made up his mind. He was going to stick around the area until the stores opened up again at six o'clock the following morning. Seven hours wasn't too long to wait. He had bottles of water in his backpack. He also had a granola bar. Ensign had three hundred and six dollars in cash in his wallet. The three hundred was from the recent sale of his gym equipment. The six was his walking-around money he had saved up in case he wanted to have a gourmet meal at a five-star restaurant on a resort somewhere. Or maybe the six was actually just what remained of all the cash Ensign had left in the world.

After twenty minutes, Ensign was no longer worn out from the walk. He stood up, put on his backpack, and began to walk further into the city from the strip malls. Ensign walked through the parking lot of an assisted-living community and continued on toward the interstate overpass which marked the boundary of Perrysburg proper. Ensign walked through the underpass, between the road and a steep ditch.

The sound of cars passing above him on the interstate brought back memories of growing up. Those cars above him, in the southbound lanes: they would be passing by the house where he grew up; just thirty seconds down that very road from that overpass. After passing the school to the right of I-75, the neighborhoods began. Ensign's childhood home, in that neighborhood on the right, had a backyard which extended to the fence separating suburbia from the hill of the interstate. Ensign, having journeyed a lifetime, was moments from his childhood. Just a stone's throw from his former life, but a million miles removed from the ghosts and memories of a life no longer there.

As Ensign approached a gas station beyond that overpass, something caught his eye. There was a different parking lot a hundred yards away, between the gas station and the hill of the overpass. There was a lone car parked in the middle of the lot. The driver's side door was wide open. Ensign could just barely see the silhouette of someone seated in the front seat. Ensign turned his head towards the gas station in front of him. He crossed the gas station parking lot, and he walked inside the store.

The clerk inside the gas station was a friendly, middle-aged woman. Ensign got a slushie and walked to the register. As he made small talk with the clerk, he asked for a single cigar. He had time, and he decided to sit on some bleachers which were set up along the side of the gas station. After a few more minutes of small talk, Ensign took his slushie and his cigar and walked out of the store. As he walked around to the small set of bleachers on the side of the building, he unstrapped his backpack. Ensign climbed up to sit on one of the benches, and he placed his backpack below him at his feet. Ensign lit the cigar as he again rested from his walk.

Accidental Art

Ensign's time in his storage unit was winding down. He didn't know how he would leave, but he knew he wasn't going to be there forever. The nights were getting cold. Ensign's paranoia had him always thinking people knew he was living there. The staff of the complex, the daily softball players and crowds, the workers at the factories at the end of the auxiliary road, the construction workers building a new structure up by the main road; Ensign was conspicuous, and he knew it. The problem: he still had nowhere else to go.

In the dark one night, Ensign's glasses broke. The frame broke in the middle, and the pieces dropped to the floor below him. Without his glasses, Ensign had trouble finding his glasses. After an hour, Ensign located both pieces of the frame and one of his lenses. There was no fixing the frame. Ensign only had one of his lenses anyhow. Things went from worst to beyond worst. All Ensign saw was blur in front of his face. To see anything, he had to hold his remaining lens up to his right eye.

Unable to see anything, Ensign made the two-mile walk to Walmart the next afternoon. He bought a pair of reading glasses and some epoxy. As he sat outside of Walmart, Ensign popped out the right lens of the readers and glued his old lens in place. The lens was all scratched up, but at least he could see again out of one eye.

On the walk back to storage, the wind picked up as Ensign traversed the terrain on the side of the state highway which led out of town. As Ensign stumbled back home, a gust of wind blew his new glasses off of his face. The grass was long, and Ensign was again unable to see. It took him twenty minutes, as the rain intensified, for Ensign to finally locate his homemade glasses amongst the grass and weeds on the side of the road. Mosquitos were terrible that evening. Ensign did all he could to bat them away as he continued his return journey to his storage home.

When Ensign reached the railroad tracks by the crossroad to Jane's house, a police cruiser flashed lights and pulled up in front of him. Ensign threw his backpack in the trunk and caught a ride back to the storage complex. When the officer typed in the gate code, which Ensign supplied, the code didn't work. Ensign realized, in that moment, that he was a day late on his monthly payment.

The officer retrieved Ensign's backpack from her trunk. As the cruiser sat at the gate, Ensign put his backpack on and began walking. He thanked the officer for the ride, and he squeezed through the gap between the fence and the gate. That was when he was abruptly told to stop.

"Are you kidding me? You can't do that right in front of me. If the code doesn't work, you don't have access. You can't go in there, that's trespassing."

"Alright, I won't. I'll sit right here and make some phone calls."

The officer drove away. It was dark outside at that point. There was no way Ensign could pay his bill until the next business day. In that moment, Ensign was effectively banned from the storage unit; his only home at the end of the 2021 summer.

"Okay, baby. I'll be there in about twenty minutes."

Ensign hung up the phone. A reprieve. Ensign had an out. Barb, an older White woman from north Toledo, was on her way to pick Ensign up from the pavement where he sat, outside the gate to the storage complex. Ensign had met Barb on an app back in 2019. The two of them had hung out, but Ensign hadn't seen her in two years. Back in the day, the two of them made a couple of videos together. Ensign was relieved that Barb was able and willing to come pick him up.

The rain stopped as Ensign sat in wait on the pavement in the night. Ensign, his backpack, and his one-sided homemade glasses were moving to Toledo. Ensign could pay his storage bill when the staff arrive on Monday morning. Barb could then bring him back to grab supplies. She had a spare room. Ensign had plenty to furnish the room. Barb was Ensign's guardian angel that night. Ensign prepared for a change of scenery. It was long overdue. Though Ensign's vision was only through a scratched single lens, he finally had a vision for a future away from the metal box.

Over the next couple of weeks, Ensign and Barb made multiple trips to retrieve items from the storage unit. Ensign spent much time in the detached garage in Barb's backyard. He cleaned it out and organized it. He put an electric motor on the scooter he bought in Bowling Green. Ensign did yardwork, and he did work around the house. He redid the glassed-in front porch. He pulled up the carpet on the main floor of the house to expose the hardwood floor underneath. Ensign fixed the stove in the kitchen. He deep cleaned and organized all the cupboards. Ensign arranged for a nonworking car to be sold for scrap.

Customizing his new bedroom with countless items from his storage unit; Ensign painted walls and hung shelves. He set up a living space similar to his old room back at Jane's house. Ensign cleaned out the shed behind the pool in the backyard. Trip after trip to Perrysburg resulted in Barb's shed being filled with items from his storage unit. The point arrived where Ensign's payments lapsed, and he lost his storage unit. Though it was still full of his belongings, his most treasured items had been moved to his room, the garage, and the shed at Barb's house.

Lex came through for Ensign once again in the first couple weeks he was living at Barb's house. She set him up an eye doctor's appointment and bought him two pairs of much needed new glasses. Ensign waited on pins and needles for three days between the appointment and the call to inform him that his glasses were ready for pickup. Ensign literally cried as Barb drove him back to the house after going to pick them up. Ensign could finally see again. His life had changed for the better.

Barb had another car parked in her driveway, her old daily-driver. It had issues running. Ensign got it working, and he began driving again. Barb put him on her car insurance, and it somehow lowered her monthly payment. Since Ensign was driving again, he began donating plasma at the donation center in north Toledo. He was able to donate twice a week and get paid for it. Ensign ran out of crystal within the first two weeks of living with Barb, and he began donating plasma the following week; with no substances in his system.

Ensign began a new regimen of working out while staying with Barb. He had saved four dumbbells from storage; four dumbbells he never sold. Daily, Ensign went out to the glassed-in front porch, turned on music, and lifted weights for a while. He felt better than he had in quite some time. Though he always maintained top shape, the new consistent workout routine added a noticeable change in a noticeably brief time.

Ensign picked up a cough in mid-November. Prone to bronchitis as a child, Ensign figured he caught bronchitis from living in Barb's home, where cigarettes were smoked indoors. Ensign hadn't been sick in any other way in six years, so the chronic cough bugged him to no end. Ensign also hadn't drunk alcohol since mid-2016. He made a choice one night. He wanted to cure his cough. He had a plan. Ensign downed an entire mid-sized bottle of vodka one night. When he woke up the next morning, his cough was gone. It worked, but it also opened a gate which had been closed long ago.

Ensign met a Black girl on an app online. She was a twenty-eight-year-old traveling nurse. When she wasn't traveling, she lived in Detroit. One snowy night, Ensign agreed to drive up to meet her at a hotel in Detroit. The drive was treacherous that night, but Ensign was happy to be driving again. Ensign and the nurse met up outside the hotel, and they went up to the room together. The scene was familiar; Ensign engaged in intimate activity with the nurse on the bed in the hotel room. It was like old times. Ensign felt free again, like he was in control of his life. It had been a while since he last felt that way; it had been since his Subaru was still running in Florida at the beginning of the year.

There were some issues with the cleanliness of the Detroit hotel room. The comforter was stained. That wasn't a big deal, though. Ensign always took hotel comforters off of the beds immediately anyhow. The concern came when Ensign looked at the floor on the side of the bed. Though Ensign and the nurse had already used the bed for their purposes, Ensign found a used condom on the floor which was not theirs.

Ensign called down to the front office. They refused to switch his room. Ensign didn't want to remain in the room any longer. The nurse was fine with remaining there in the contaminated room. Somehow, the conversation between Ensign and the nurse became heated. After a few minutes, Ensign made a decision. He told the nurse he was leaving, and he gathered up his belongings and left.

It was still snowing in the middle of the night when Ensign left the hotel. He couldn't see the lane markings on the road due to snow coverage. Ensign turned left towards the highway from a non-turn lane at an intersection. The police officer behind him switched direction to pull him over along the side of the road. Ensign explained what had happened. The officer told him to be careful, and he sent Ensign on his way.

Ensign reconnected with his friend Makayla in the fall of 2021. Some days, like old times, Ensign would go pick her up from her grandma's house. The two of them would go pick up cocaine and return to Barb's garage for the night to do drugs and interact intimately. Makayla sniffed the drug, and Ensign shot it. Though it wasn't crystal, Ensign got by from shooting up the coke with forty-five-minute gaps between shots. As the Sun came up in the early mornings, Ensign and Makayla came down from the drugs and ceased their sexual interactions. Ensign would then return Makayla to her grandma's house on the other side of Toledo.

On other days, Makayla's uncle came and picked up Ensign. On those days, Ensign bought crack. That was the drug of choice at Makayla's uncle's house in inner-city Toledo. Random women were sometimes passed out on the couches. At other times, they would all be seated around the dining room table. Everyone played dice games and cards as the crack pipe made its way around the circle for hours on end. Makayla's uncle was a friendly guy. Ensign always felt welcome on those days, having cookouts and drug-fueled fun.

Ensign's friend Alyssa, still in contact since Ensign first mistook her for Jane in the Perrysburg Kroger parking lot, visited Ensign as well. Some days, they did crystal and coke in Toledo. Other times, they went back to Alyssa's house in Rossford to get high. Ensign liked Alyssa. She was friendly and beautiful. He never caught a vibe from her for anything more than friendship, so he kept respectful and never made a move. Had Alyssa instigated anything, Ensign would have been receptive. Though Ensign didn't quite understand his dynamic with Alyssa, he valued it for whatever it was.

Ensign also reconnected with his friend Betsy during the time he stayed at Barb's house in late 2021. Betsy, as Ensign had hoped, was still using crystal. She had remained away from crack cocaine that entire time since Ensign first introduced her to crystal as an alternative. Betsy and Ensign met up on occasions. Since Betsy was driving, she sometimes drove to hang out with Ensign in Barb's garage. At other times, Ensign drove to where she was staying in Point Place, a tip of Toledo on the shore of Lake Erie.

Betsy chose an odd place to meet Ensign one night. Ensign had been past the location countless times. He had even been inside that particular adult video store on occasions in the past. He couldn't understand why Betsy was so insistent that they met at midnight in the parking lot of the store. Ensign, as usual, was paranoid. Was it a setup? Ensign, despite knowing Betsy for multiple decades, was apprehensive about meeting her there.

After some pressure, Ensign gave in and agreed to the midnight meetup at the adult video store. He didn't have any drugs, so he figured nothing could go wrong. Ensign knew that by seeing Betsy, it was his way to get high on crystal that night. He pulled into the parking lot and parked next to Betsy's car. Betsy handed Ensign the glass stem when he sat down in her car. After the two of them smoked crystal for a few minutes, Ensign asked the question which was burning in his mind.

"So, why were you so insistent on meeting me in this particular parking lot?"

"Get out of the car, and I'll show you."

Betsy led Ensign to the far side of the storefront. She stopped in front of a nondescript door on the side of the building. Though Ensign had been inside the store before, he had only ever used the main entrance to come and go. Ensign had seen the door before. He figured it led to a storage area, or something. He honestly never put too much thought into what was behind the door. Betsy knocked on the door. Suddenly, Ensign began wondering what was on the other side.

The door opened. A middle-aged man waved Betsy and Ensign inside. He closed the door behind them. The three of them were then standing in a square room, empty of any furniture besides a single folding chair. Ensign saw another door on the opposite side of the room. Just then, the middle-aged man motioned that Betsy and Ensign were good to step through the other door.

Ensign wondered what was going on. He wondered what he had just walked into. Ensign eyed the man standing in the room with them. The man smiled back, but he didn't speak a word. Betsy was already through the door as Ensign slowly stepped past the man to follow her into the darkness beyond the threshold of the doorway. Once Ensign was through the door with Betsy, the man closed the door behind them.

"What is this place?"

"You're about to see. I've been here a few times. I've wanted to show you since I first came here."

Ensign was not expecting what he saw inside that building. There were multiple rooms branching off from a hallway which continued down to what Ensign assumed was the back of the building. Betsy led Ensign through the side rooms. The rooms were dark, random lights of different colors partially illuminated different rooms. Every room had a BDSM theme of its own; platforms with leather restraints, exam chairs with shackles, one room had chains of different length hanging from different locations in the ceiling.

Ensign's mind flashed back to the farmhouse outside of Lansing, Michigan. That homeowner took so much pride in his creation as he showed Ensign around. Ensign had been impressed back in Lansing. The craftsmanship, the art, the setup; it was amazing. That weird building in Toledo where Betsy had brought him; it was the exact opposite.

That building in Toledo was grimy. The vibe, felt immediately upon entrance, was creepy. The holes in the walls, the dilapidated and exposed wood, the burns and damage to the shoddy upholstery; no upkeep had been done to any of the interior. The air smelled stale, there was a humidity, and the moisture felt like sweat on Ensign's skin. Bad things and body heat had worked up an atmosphere like a swamp in that enclosed space. Ensign felt gross just being inside the building.

Betsy and Ensign weren't the only two people inside that secret Toledo BDSM building. There were six others inside, paired off in three of the six rooms along the hallway. As the couples Engaged in erotic activity, Betsy led Ensign to a room at the back of the hallway. Ensign heard sex noises as he walked past the rooms which contained people engaging in sexual activity. He heard other noises as well; the sounds of hands smacking bare skin.

As Ensign stood in that room, far from the entrance at the opposite end of the hallway, he looked at Betsy. Ensign then glanced to a wooden structure bolted to the floor in the middle of the room. He took note of the restraints attached to the wooden platform. Ensign turned to face Betsy again. For some reason, Betsy looked excited as she gazed back at him. Ensign opened his mouth to speak.

"Okay, that's it for me. Let's go. I feel dirty just standing here."

In late 2021, Betsy was dating someone up in Detroit. He was the source of her crystal. Since Ensign had no immediate source at that moment, Betsy hooked him up on the random occasions they saw each other. One evening, Ensign and Betsy had been texting back-and-forth. Betsy agreed to come pick Ensign up so they could make a run to Detroit together to get high. Betsy pulled up out front, and Ensign hopped in her car. They were off to Detroit.

Betsy was irritable on the entire drive. She was short with Ensign when he spoke to her. She yelled about things and ranted about nothing. Ensign felt confused, but he sat back for the ride. After an hour and some backtracking, the two of them reached the proper exit to the inner city. At that point, Betsy was even angrier due to initially missing the proper exit and having to turn around. Betsy pulled into the parking lot of a seedy gas station in the middle of the night. The area, as Ensign knew, was rough.

It was only at that point that Betsy told Ensign he wouldn't be able to travel the rest of the way with her to her guy's house. She told Ensign he had to get out of the car. She said things would instantly go bad if her guy even suspected someone rode with her to his house. Ensign didn't like the situation at all. He realized he didn't have a choice. Ensign stepped out of the car to wait outside the gas station. Though it was the middle of the night, people were out and about on foot and in cars.

Ensign did his best to blend in, as the token White guy in that area of Detroit. He bought a bag of chips and a coffee inside the gas station. After he slid his money under the glass which separated him from the cashier, he went back outside to dodge homeless people, and to ignore glares from drivers at the gas pump. Ensign stayed outside against the wall of the gas station for well over an hour. He was getting very impatient when Betsy finally returned to pick him up.

Ensign expected to receive an eightball. What he got was just under a gram. Betsy, Ensign's lifelong friend, someone he had hooked up countless times before, had ripped him off. Ensign remained silent on the drive back to Toledo. As he got out of her car, he told Betsy that their interactions were done. He wanted restitution, and that was that. As Betsy tried to apologize to him, Ensign shut the door to her car and walked away.

Since Lex moved back from Manhattan earlier in the year to live with her parents and help them out, Ensign stopped over at their house on occasions to eat dinner. Other times, Lex and Ensign met up to eat lunch at a Mexican restaurant between Barb's house and Lex's parent's house. Both homes were close to each other in north Toledo. They were about two miles apart. Ensign was happy to frequently see his friend Lex again. Prior to the fall of 2021, Ensign hadn't seen Lex since he stayed with her in Manhattan, right before the coronavirus pandemic became a thing.

As December progressed, the urge to travel weighed heavily on Ensign's mind. Ensign did crystal occasionally with friends of his. He drank alcohol occasionally at Barb's house. Since the cold winter began, Ensign shifted from hanging out in the detached garage to staying in his bedroom inside the house. Ensign had a lot on his mind. He resumed online interactions with people all around the country. Ensign's time at Barb's house was going as well as expected, but he couldn't shake the urge to explore. With nothing holding him in place, Ensign was free to go where he pleased.

Though Ensign had remained in contact with his friend and former client, David; he hadn't seen David since one day when he returned to Michigan from down in Georgia in mid-2019. As exhausted as he was from lack of sleep and the drive north, Ensign still chose to tan in the booth in David's basement. Ensign fell asleep under the new bulbs for half an hour. When he awoke, he was so sunburnt that he had to spend the next three days lying perfectly still on the bed in a basement bedroom.

Much time had passed, and David's life had changed. When Ensign visited David in the past, he went to the house which David shared with his husband. In fall of 2021, David was single. David also sold his house earlier in the year. Ensign found out he was living with his mother up in Ann Arbor.

Ensign and David made plans to reconnect one evening. David drove down and picked Ensign up from Barb's house. The two of them went out to eat at a sandwich restaurant and caught up on life together. When David dropped Ensign off at Barb's house later that night, he handed Ensign a small bag of crystal. Though it wasn't much, Ensign was appreciative of the gesture. He was then able to remain high for the next few days.

Remaining high was important during those days at barb's house in the very beginning of 2022. Ensign had set into motion his thoughts of travel. He had new plans in place, and he needed the extra energy from crystal to manage what he needed to do to put his plans into action. Online, Ensign had met a girl on an app. She was a twenty-six-year-old Asian woman who lived in Fresno, California. Ensign and Mia grew extremely close in a brief period of time. They texted, they talked on the phone, and they shared video calls.

Weeks passed; the holiday season of 2021 became the dawn of 2022. Ensign was drinking beer one evening with Barb, and he spilled out his plans for the future. Barb hadn't expected to hear what Ensign told her, and Ensign hadn't planned to tell her in the way he did. He was going to tell her eventually, but alcohol may have preemptively loosened his tongue that evening. Ensign was happy to put the words out there. It was another weight lifted off his shoulders.

"So, here's the thing; I'm going to be leaving soon. My friend Lex bought me an airline ticket. I'm heading out to California."

"What, really? You have people out there?"

"Yeah, I'm going to see how it goes. I can't shake the urge to travel. I appreciate being able to stay here. You literally rescued me from the side of the road, and I'll be grateful forever. I also appreciate being able to keep my belongings in your shed out back."

"Well, thank you for the work you did around here. Having you here was…interesting, to say the least."

"I love ya, Barb."

"Love you, too…"

Ensign hugged Barb. He could feel the awkwardness in the air despite having a buzz from the alcohol. The two of them continued to drink together that evening, but Barb was quieter than usual. Ensign felt bad for unloading that new information on her like that, but he knew he needed to tell her sooner rather than later.

Ensign had a lot to do before he left. He needed to completely clear out his bedroom, stocked full of belongings. He then needed to paint the walls and fill in all the holes from the shelves and decorations he had hung up. He needed to pack as carefully as he could for the flight to California, and he needed to put everything else in the shed out back. Ensign's bedroom at Barb's house, same as his storage unit had been, was overloaded with way too many items. Ensign was going to need the crystal David had given him. It was going to be the fuel to work around the clock until it was time to leave. Ensign knew he needed as much time as possible because of how much work he needed to complete.

Preparation

The ceiling fan in Ensign's bedroom; it was the bane of his time living with Barb. Barb had many projects around the house when Ensign moved in. Ensign completed every one of them in his time there…except for one. The old ceiling fan was broken long before Ensign's arrival. The new ceiling fan was packed in the closet of Ensign's bedroom. Though he made attempts to replace the old fan with the new one, he never successfully finished out the job. The wiring and the brackets seemed straightforward. Ensign, high on crystal, needed to give it one more try. Ensign, still high on crystal and having been electrocuted twice, decided to settle for installing the fan in the ceiling without connecting the wires.

The fan ended up in place, bracketed securely to the ceiling. The wiring was capped off. Ensign left it at that, form over function. It looked better than the previous fan, and it functioned exactly the same as the old fan functioned; it didn't. Twice, the house went dark as Ensign fell off of a chair in the middle of the bedroom. Twice, Ensign received burns to his fingers. Twice, Ensign thought that the electricity to the room was turned off, and he still got shocked. Twice, Ensign had to flip the circuit breaker to restore power to the house. There was not going to be a strike three. Ensign's crystal-inspired need to finish the job was cooked out of him. It was the only job Ensign failed to complete for Barb.

For the rest of the room, Ensign felt as overwhelmed as he had when he began sorting his old storage unit. He knew the irony of the situation. All of the items he was about to pack up and remove from his bedroom, they were all items he had repeatedly sorted, time and time again, back in his storage unit. The same items, just less of them. The same belongings, just with less garbage and broken things. The same task, just with a definite and limited timeline. The hoard was inescapable. When Ensign left the hoard, the hoard relocated with him, trip by trip and carload by carload.

During that last week in Ohio at Barb's house, as expected, crystal was an absolute requirement for the around-the-clock work that was needed to wrap up his stay at the house. Days and nights passed in a blur. Half of the time, Ensign wasn't even sure if it was light outside or dark. He would find out when he managed to get boxes sorted out enough to run them out to the shed in the backyard. Sorting, packing, painting; Ensign barely took breaks to eat, and he never slept.

His focus, obsessive and compulsive, bordered on destructive to his physical health. He felt his body breaking down from lack of food and rest, but he kept going. At one point, he suddenly lost his senses of smell and taste. Lex had texted Ensign that she had contracted coronavirus, so had David. Ensign assumed he did too, but he pressed on. He didn't care about anything except the task at hand, and he was going to finish before his flight.

Ensign finally completed the work. The room was empty. The walls were freshly painted. Ensign curled up on the floor and fell asleep. His small supply of crystal had lasted through the job, but it ran out right at the end. It was good timing, and he didn't care. He planned to head to California drug-free, anyhow. Ensign had two suitcases and a backpack in the corner of his empty room. It was all he was going to take with him across the country. It was enough, and the rest of his belongings, the items saved from his doomed storage unit, were loaded into the shed behind Barb's pool. The shed, like the storage unit, was filled completely. Ensign was done.

After some issues with the airline the day before he was planning to leave, Lex sent Ensign the money to cover the difference in ticket prices. Ensign spent that entire day on the phone with the airline. The stress was high as Ensign tried to sort out the situation. Though Ensign had confirmation that he previously purchased his ticket, nothing was showing up for his flight when he looked up the details. His earlier purchase, unbeknownst to him, hadn't been confirmed by the airline. Ensign then needed the money to cover the difference for a short-notice ticket.

After that ordeal, and Lex coming to the rescue again, Ensign was finally in the clear. All the work around the house had been completed. Ensign's flight was guaranteed. All he had to do was wait. With nothing to do to stay busy, Ensign's mind went to dark places. Whether it was his depression, withdrawal from drugs, or a combination of the two, Ensign was in a bad place mentally.

Ensign drank alcohol alone in the empty bedroom on the day he was to leave for the airport. Barb was at work until three thirty that afternoon. Ensign drank as he waited for her to get home. He stared at the walls and wondered about the uncertainty ahead. Ensign thought about all that could go wrong. He thought about all of the negative which befell him over the previous year. Though Ensign was excited for a new adventure, fear of his life once again falling apart was at the forefront of his mind. However ready he thought he was, he knew, deep down, that he wasn't.

It was gray and depressing outside when Barb walked in from work. While she changed into different clothes, Ensign loaded his luggage into her car. It was freezing outside, and snow was falling lightly. Ensign looked around. It was the last day he was going to be at Barb's home in Ohio. He was about to face the unknown. Ensign closed up the car door and walked back inside. He had some beer he was planning to drink on the ride. He needed to step back into Barb's house to grab it.

"You ready? Did you get all your stuff loaded up? Even with weather and traffic, we should make good time to Detroit."

"I just need to grab these beers…There, I'm ready."

Ensign wasn't ready, and he knew it.

Anhedonia

"Well...this is it."

"Barb, seriously, thank you for everything. Thanks for saving me that night, thanks for the storage shed, thanks for letting me stay at your home."

"Well, I wish you the best out there. Stay on the right path."

"I will. I don't know what's about to happen, but it's my time. Be safe driving back."

Ensign wiped a tear from his eye, and he closed the door to Barb's car. The snow was falling hard, and the wind had picked up, as Ensign walked into the terminal of the Detroit airport. It was almost dark outside. Ensign looked around for a clock. It was just past six o'clock in the evening. Ensign was hungry, and the effects of the beers he drank had all but worn off, leaving him tired and groggy. Ensign knew how his night was about to go. He had accepted his fate well before he stepped into the terminal at the airport. Ensign had a long night ahead of him. His flight didn't depart until eleven o'clock the following morning.

Ensign checked in at the airline desk. He asked where he could get some food. The woman behind the counter told him that all the places which sold food outside of the gates had closed at six o'clock. Ensign asked if he could get through the gates so he could eat. He found out that he had to wait until two hours prior to takeoff to cross through the gates. Once the woman behind the counter saw when Ensign's flight was scheduled to depart, she took pity on him.

"Tell ya what. I get an employee meal on my shift. You can

have it. I'll run inside at get it for you. Is a chicken Caesar salad alright?"

"Yes, absolutely. Thank you so much."

Ensign rolled his two new suitcases over to a row of seats along a wall of glass windows. He took off his jacket to use as a pillow and put his feet up on his bags. Ensign took his headphones and his phone out of his backpack. Moments later, true to her word, Ensign had a large plastic bowl in front of him. Still deep in a downward spiral of thought, Ensign ate his meal as he glanced around at all the people inside the airport. Everyone living their own unique lives, people heading from here to there, wrapped up in everything consuming their own unique worlds; Ensign was so different from everyone else he saw, and everyone else was so different from all the others.

Through the night, Ensign watched movies on his phone. He remained in a constant battle with getting comfortable. The rigid plastic seats and armrests left little room to find a position which was comfortable for more than a few minutes. The longer he sat, the harder it was to stay seated. New people came and went around him. Workers behind the counter, in the distance, were replaced with the next shift of airline employees. Commuters hurrying past were soon gone, out of Ensign's life on their own journeys through the world. New people passed by in other directions, on to their own unique life experiences. Ensign sat and watched, seated there for the duration.

Ensign jolted awake the next morning. Sunlight from the early morning had begun to fill the terminal where he sat. He was amazed that he managed to get some sleep, but it wasn't much. His neck hurt from sleeping upright in a chair. It was still early; Ensign could tell from the light. He checked his phone; it was eight thirty. In half an hour, he would be able to head through the gates and into the inner terminal.

Ensign waited in line with his bags at the main security checkpoint. Slowly, the line moved forward. As people placed their personal effects on the conveyor belt to the x-ray machine, others stepped through the body scanner. Ensign reached the point where he had to remove his shoes. He put them in a bin with his backpack. He put the smaller of his two suitcases up on the belt behind his backpack. He had bag-checked his larger suitcase before he stepped into the security line.

Ensign stepped through the body scanner. He then walked back over to the belt to take his belongings from the other side of the x-ray machine. His items came out on the belt. As he pulled his backpack and suitcase from the belt, an employee took the bin with his shoes and wallet. Security again placed the bin in front of the x-ray machine to run it through a second time. Ensign wondered what was going on. After the third time, Ensign asked what was happening.

Ensign felt a jolt of adrenaline as he remembered something from long ago. Ensign's mind flashed back to an extremely specific moment in time. It was almost Halloween in 2020. The sparkle of the Sun's reflection caught Ensign's attention as he stood outside of his Subaru on the side of the road in Aurora, Colorado. Ensign walked back to his Lexus, parked behind his Subaru. Ensign opened the door on the driver's side and reached in to remove the source of the light's reflection.

In that moment, as he stood next to security at the airport in Detroit, Ensign knew what was going on. Ensign looked across toward the offices beyond the far wall of the security checkpoint. As he watched, an airline security employee pointed back in his direction. Ensign saw a Detroit police officer step out from the office and follow the security worker back over to where Ensign was standing. The oversight, clear as day in retrospect, was burning in Ensign's mind as he waited for the inevitable police interaction.

"Oh, my God. I know what's going on. I'm so sorry. I forgot that it was even in there. It's been in my wallet since I had to leave my car in Colorado last year. I'm moving to California right now. I..."

Ensign once again began to explain his situation to yet another police officer at rapid-fire speed. The officer held up a finger as he opened up Ensign's wallet. Ensign couldn't believe what was happening. He was so close, so close to being on his way. He had made it through being stranded in Florida, then stuck in Texas, then he was left for a day in the middle of Illinois. He made it through the worst point in his life, stranded in a storage unit in his hometown for weeks on end. He just spent the previous week wrapping up loose ends at Barb's house. He spent a day on the phone with the airline to fix issues with his booking, and he spent a full night on a plastic seat in the airport.

Ensign was so close. All he had to do was walk through the terminal to reach his gate, sit down, and wait for the airline to announce boarding of the aircraft. He was less than two hours away from beginning a new chapter of his life. Ensign came so far to reach that moment. It was less than two hours away...and an easily avoidable oversight may have just ruined everything.

Durability

The last item Ensign retrieved from his Lexus on the side of the road in Aurora, Colorado in late 2020; Ensign had forgotten about it. He bought it at a mall in Toledo back when he was a teenager. From the time he began driving, Ensign always had it with him. Anytime Ensign switched cars, he made sure that it was hung from the rearview mirror of his latest vehicle. It was nothing that caught any negative attention in a car. Ensign hadn't thought twice about it since he took it from his Lexus and slipped it into his wallet. Ensign forgot about it after that.

Ensign never hung it in his Subaru because he forgot he had it. It stayed with him, in his wallet, as he traveled the country by car, and by bus, in 2021. It stayed in his wallet as he spent the night in the airport in Detroit, and it was with him as he waited in the security line to enter the terminal gates. It went through the metal detector when Ensign tossed his wallet in the bin on the conveyor belt…and then it was run through the machine two more times by a security worker. That third time through the x-ray machine was what prompted Ensign to remember he had it. At that point, it was out of his control.

When that Detroit police officer pulled it from Ensign's wallet, all Ensign could do was nod. There, held up in front of him, was the little metal ninja star Ensign bought at the mall as a teenager. Ensign knew it wasn't an appropriate airline carry-on item. He knew he was potentially facing an issue. Ensign decided to open his big fat mouth.

"Dude, I seriously forgot that was even in there. I took it from my car when it broke down in Colorado. I haven't even thought about it since then. It's not a weapon, I promise."

"Well, this could be an issue...but I don't think it's a weapon..."

Ensign, on autopilot, began to recite his story another time. "Seriously, it's not. I'm moving to California right now. I've been here in the airport since last night. I'm down on my luck. I'm headed out there to start over..."

The officer cut him off. "I have to take this from you. I need you to sign this paper stating you acknowledge we confiscated this item from you while you were entering through security. This could catch you a charge. I could take you to jail, but I don't think all that needs to happen."

"Thank you, sir. I'm sorry I had that with me. I seriously forgot."

Ensign stepped off to the side and put his shoes on as quickly as he could. The fog of the embarrassment, and the adrenaline of the situation, slowly wore off as Ensign walked through the airport terminal. He was through that last hurdle before the new life ahead of him. Ensign found the proper gate, and he sat down to wait for his flight.

Hours later, on Mountain Time, Ensign stepped into the terminal of the airport in Denver, Colorado. The winter weather was horrible; the short walk down the steps of the airplane, across the runway, and into the building froze Ensign to the core. Instantly, Ensign was able to warm up. He had under an hour until his next flight, so he had to pick up the pace to reach the far side of the Denver terminal. There was a lot of ground to cover, and Ensign was dripping sweat just moments after he escaped the outside cold of Colorado in January. Though he wasn't running, his pace was fast enough that he had to frequently stop and catch his breath.

On one of Ensign's short breaks, Ensign stripped off his coat. As he wiped sweat from his forehead, Ensign checked his location. He made it. After crossing the airport, Ensign found his departure gate. Just as he slumped down into a seat to wait, the call to board his flight came across the intercom. Ensign wasn't going to be able to pick up any food to satiate his growing hunger, but he was at least going to make his connecting flight to California.

On Pacific Time, hours later, Ensign arrived in Fresno, California. The airport was decorated to showcase the wilderness of the Yosemite National Forrest. Ensign walked through the terminal, amongst the large fake sequoia trees lining the inside of the terminal walkways. Just before Ensign entered the baggage claim area, he walked through a massive base of a fake sequoia tree; a tunnel designed to replicate the real tunnels for vehicles on the roads in the area.

The actual tree tunnels were carved through real sequoia trees growing in that part of California. Even the scaled-down walking tunnel, through the fake tree in the airport, was impressive. Ensign did a little research on his phone. Yosemite National Park was a mere half hour from where Mia lived. Ensign hoped he would get the chance to see the actual sequoia trees in the near future. Though the nature artwork inside the airport in Fresno was impressive, Ensign had no energy left in him to truly appreciate his situation.

Ensign wanted to be away from airports for a while. Fresno, the third and final airport of the day, was almost just a memory. Ensign reached baggage claim. After some waiting, he scooped up his suitcase as it popped out on the conveyor belt. Ensign, with all of his luggage, stepped out into the warm California night. The weather was perfect: no precipitation, a nice temperature, a cool breeze.

The cold winter of the Midwest was gone. The freezing Colorado snowstorm was behind him. There were no more airports in Ensign's immediate future. Ensign took a deep breath. He exhaled slowly as he looked around at the line of cars waiting to pick people up from the terminal. All he had to do was locate Mia's car, and his latest journey would be complete. As Ensign began to walk towards the cars, he felt something else. Originally, Ensign first thought it was just stress. He realized what it was as he looked for Mia; Ensign was beginning to go through drug withdrawal.

California Knows How to Party

Ensign knew Mia was drug free. Ensign wanted to live drug free with her in California. The ghosts from his immediate past were interfering with Ensign's goals. From the time Ensign ran out of drugs, when he finished packing up his room at Barb's house, he was distracted by immediate concerns. It wasn't until he stepped out from the airport, into the California night, that all of those stressors were suddenly lifted. At that moment, with a clear mind, Ensign knew he was about to face a horrible mental and physical transition to sobriety.

Timing doomed Ensign from the very beginning. All those things which should have been magical first moments; meeting Mia for the first time, their first hug and kiss, riding with her back to her house, seeing the decorations Mia set up to welcome Ensign into her home; all of the magic from those first experiences was shrouded in an ever-growing fog of drug withdrawal. Ensign knew that if he could just wait for it to pass, over the next couple of days, he would come out on the other side and be able to progress his new dynamic. From what he knew from his exchanges with Mia, Ensign was fairly certain that she wouldn't understand. Ensign, in that moment, decided he was going to keep the drug withdrawal to himself.

Mental and physical exhaustion, with no chemicals to boost energy, left Ensign in a constant fog of lethargy. He could barely complete thoughts. Ensign slept while Mia went to work. He slept while she was home. Mia went about her days while Ensign remained in bed. Depression, when Ensign was awake, caused him to wish he was asleep. Thoughts were hard to keep in his head; he didn't have the energy to try to think.

Mia checked on Ensign, and Ensign responded with new complaints of aches and pains. Ensign never let Mia know what was going on, he just hoped it would pass before she had enough of him. Mia tried to initiate intimacy. Ensign brushed off any advances. If she lay down on the bed next to him, Ensign rolled over to face the other direction. All of Mia's efforts caused her frustration, Ensign could tell. Ensign wasn't in any condition to fix his failing dynamic.

Four days passed. Ensign was miserable. He knew Mia was unhappy. He heard her on the phone with her parents: arguing about moving back into their house to help take care of her father. Ensign just needed to get through the withdrawal. Ensign thought of ways to help. He picked a terrible way to try and remedy the situation.

Ensign made a suggestion to Mia. He told her he wanted to get drunk with her. Mia was all for it. She didn't know Ensign's history with alcohol. She thought it was going to be fun. Ensign just wanted some relief from his withdrawal symptoms. Ensign figured his time was almost up. Having heard Mia discussing her move back to her parents' house, he knew she had an excuse to give him the boot. He knew that his stay was coming to an end. Ensign knew alcohol wasn't going to be a good thing, but he had lost all hope of making that situation with Mia work. Ensign felt terrible in every way, and he wanted it to end.

The January days in Fresno, California were seventy degrees and sunny. Ensign squinted as he stepped out of Mia's front door. It was the first time he had left the house since he showed up. Mia lived in a neighborhood of townhouses in the middle of fields. Mia lived in wine country. Mia's block, a collection of similar townhouses, was visible in all directions from the fields of grapes; one square block of homes which seemed to be placed in the middle of nowhere.

When Ensign and Mia reached the grocery store, Mia led Ensign to the back of the store. There in the back, amongst the beverage coolers, was the alcohol section. Ensign, in that moment, made a bad decision. The small bottles of whisky were ten dollars apiece. Ensign silently debated for a moment with himself. First, he had two bottles in his hands. He picked up a third bottle. Ensign looked at the three bottles in his hands. Three was the magic number. Ensign walked over to Mia. She had a pack of four hard seltzers. The two of them paid for their alcohol and left the store.

Back at the house, Ensign's mind was all over the place. The sense of impending doom was with him from the drug withdrawal, and it was amplified by his knowledge that Mia planned to move back home with her parents. Ensign opened the first pint of whiskey. Five seconds later, it was empty. Before the alcohol hit, Ensign opened the second bottle. He downed that second bottle just as fast as he had the first. As the effects of the alcohol began to take hold, Ensign opened the third bottle of liquor…

It was dark outside. What time was it? Ensign saw the digital readout from a clock. He squinted to read it; it was four o'clock in the morning. Ensign was lying naked in a bed. It was Mia's bed, but Ensign was alone. What day was it? Ensign felt like he had been out for multiple days. Ensign reached his hand around him on the bed to try to find his phone. When his fingers brushed over his phone, he picked it up and looked at the screen. Ensign saw the date on his phone screen. It was, in fact, two days later; two days had passed since he last remembered opening that third bottle of whiskey. Ensign, with one eye open, checked his text messages. He had a new message from Mia.

"We need to talk when I get home from work."

As Ensign set his phone down again, he closed his eyes. Ensign felt bad from the hangover, but he also felt better; he was on the other side of the drug withdrawal. He knew he was too late. Ensign knew the conversation was coming. Bits and pieces of memories from the previous two days flashed through Ensign's mind as he lay alone in Mia's bed. Ensign recalled tattooing himself in Mia's kitchen. He remembered kissing Mia while they were in the shower together.

Maybe nothing crazy happened while he was blacked out. Oh, no. Another memory flashed through his head; Ensign remembered a quick snippet of taking his shirt off while inside a fast-food restaurant. Then another flash of memory: walking shirtless along the fields of grapes in the California countryside. He was shirtless in that recollection...but was he also without his pants? He was fully naked when he awoke in Mia's bed...

The talk with Mia went exactly as Ensign had expected. Mia filled in the gaps in Ensign's timeline where his own drunken memory lapsed. A feeling washed over Ensign as he listened to Mia recount the events of the previous two days. It was that same feeling which he last felt in mid-2016; it was a mix of embarrassment and recollection. That feeling was one of the main reasons Ensign knew, all those years prior, that he had to completely stop drinking.

Ensign hated those conversations; each time someone told him of a drunken act, his brain suddenly registered the scene and remembered more of what had been lost in the blackout. Ensign's embarrassment grew with each newly recovered, assisted memory. As the conversation continued, as more memories were brought to the surface, Ensign's regret and embarrassment intensified.

After Mia helped Ensign piece together his two-day drunken misadventure, she followed up with the anther part to the conversation. Ensign had been awaiting that inevitable piece of information. Ensign had been correct; Mia's parents had convinced her to move back into their home to help out; amidst the failing health of her father. In Ensign's situation, he wasn't even able to blame timing for the failure. Ensign rightfully blamed himself for his failure in California.

It was Ensign's misguided wishful thinking which led him across the country as 2022 began. Ensign couldn't have seriously thought the dynamic was possible, had he considered anything beyond the desire to leave northwest Ohio yet again. It wasn't the timing with Mia's family situation, it wasn't the drug withdrawal upon his arrival, and it wasn't the drunken blackout over the prior two days.

It was Ensign; he had no good plan to make anything work, and he had no hope of that particular life becoming a reality in California...and he knew it as he flew out to Mia anyhow. Ensign had acted impulsively. He had acted in reaction to his unhappiness in northwest Ohio, and however he managed to escape that unhappiness was as far of a plan as he put in place. Ensign manipulated an out from the Midwest, and he never bothered to consider anything besides changing his immediate situation.

Ensign had failed again, and he very much deserved to fail. Ensign was through the withdrawal. He was out the other side. His hangover had worn off by the time Mia arrived home from work. All that remained was the shame and embarrassment of his entire time spent with Mia since she picked him up from the airport. Ensign failed her since he first saw her in the line of cars outside of baggage claim. Ensign had failed her from the moment the dynamic began online at the end of 2021.

Ensign's first real-world interaction with Mia had been on the half-hour car ride from the airport to her house. Ensign's last interaction with Mia was about to be that same drive, but in the opposite direction. No, Ensign didn't have a flight departing from that airport, but he also knew he was in no position to protest the return drive through the fields of grapes.

Ensign remained silent on that ride to the far side of Fresno. Ensign had his two suitcases in the back seat. Mia parked in a parking space at a hotel, along the road to the airport. She stepped from her car as Ensign got out on his side. Ensign pulled his suitcase from the back seat. Mia walked around to his side and handed him the handle to his other suitcase. Mia spoke as she gave Ensign a hug.

"Get a room here. Figure out what you are going to do."

"No, I'm not getting a room. I have no money, and I don't want a room."

As Mia began to protest, Ensign broke off the hug and turned his back on her. With one suitcase rolling on either side of him, Ensign walked away from Mia's car. Though he didn't hear Mia start her car, or leave, he didn't bother to turn back. He knew it was his own failure which resulted in the end of that short dynamic.

Ensign was alone in California. He had no money, he had no shelter, he had nowhere to go...so Ensign just walked. So many bad situations befell Ensign in 2021, each one proving more difficult than the one before it. As 2021 progressed, Ensign continued to reach new lows and drag along, in those lows, until his situation changed. That was the thing; nothing lasted forever. Life always changed. Through all the negativity, Ensign had still made it through 2021. That year was over.

2022 had begun.

Postscript

It was simple. It was needed. It grew into something. My original deal in the fall of 2018: "I can't kill myself until I write a book."

That original idea was somewhat of an excuse at a desperate time in my life. On that day in 2018, I grasped anything to give purpose to a life which I felt had no point. I made that deal to write while half-sure I was just putting off evaluating my place in my mind, and in the world around me. Amazed, as I wrote years later; I actually followed through.

It took me a long time to reach a point where I was in the right place, time, and mental space to start the actual writing. It just wasn't possible to include everything. Some of what was included were high stakes (in my own little world). Other items may seem trivial and benign, but they were included organically. I left out stories which could have sounded more exciting, or action packed...omitted as part of the process.

For each story, ten more tales went untold. The stories came out as they did...as they were meant to come out. Those stories, from exciting to the most trivial; a testament to the way my mind works. The moments during the writing process were as important to conveying the story as was the story itself. The moments of recollection and creation then combined with the original experiences and became all of my story.

I included, of course, the essential items which allowed the story of my life to progress onto (and into) other things. Other stories flowed out as I wrote. What came out, came out naturally. "Word puke." I had trouble keeping up with it at times. Once the words were out, the feelings and the stories came together in front of me.

I felt a sense of creation, words existed in an order which conveyed those recalled thoughts...thoughts otherwise jumbled up in my mind. I wonder how much in my mind, from my past, now plays a role in my current thought processes and actions. The feeling of creation through writing takes me up with each step, building from the previous step. Each memory opens a door to another memory. Sometimes, it's hard to keep up with the pace of the flow. It flows when the door is open. It comes effortlessly in those pure moments where I am nothing but a conduit. It branches off in all directions, leaving me trying to keep up with the pace. The process humbles me.

Some of what I wrote was eye-opening; I had to truly examine and evaluate decisions I made (and where I thought my head was at) in the past. I look back on those times, through those years from 2018, as if I am recalling memories from a person lost to time. A memory of someone who no longer exists. The resulting experiences, which came from each decision, made me into a new and ever-changing person, wiser in some ways; knowing the results which I had yet to see before my thoughts and subsequent actions progressed my life to new points. Those points: points to which I could never return. Those points: points before life continued forward. This paragraph, an example of how words sometimes can't convey the thoughts I try to put to words.

I learned a lot in this writing process. I learned how my current mindset affects the tone (and the take) of the stories as my brain recalls experiences from my past. It's like I am a partner with my old self, a person no longer there, someone who once existed in that life...and my current self recalls and interprets as I write, sharing a present tense take on prior events.

I think how all the experiences which have occurred came together to where I am, right now in an exact moment. Things could have been different in infinite ways. At the same time, I always have to be exactly me, exactly where I am, in an exact moment. It's a lot to wrap my head around. I fall short many times. The more I write, the more I understand. The more I understand, the more I know I understand less than I thought I understood.

I have been on as much of a journey authoring these books as I had been living out the experiences of which I wrote. Through the writing, I feel a continuation of these stories as they maintain an existence. Writing about my experiences continues the experiences in a way I didn't ever consider. My mind, occupied with thoughts, as tangible an item now as were the experiences then.

I tried to share all of me; thoughts, actions, responses, lessons, growth, stagnation, backtracking, failure, transgressions, aspirations, rifts between hopes and reality, progress...my take as I move in a world my own. Everyone lives in a world made up of input gained through individual senses and their inputs to an individual brain. My world is like no one else's. I can only see the world as my world which I move in while I exist...and I can only share my experiences, in the ways I am capable, to transfer information.

2018, 2019, and 2020 were like no other years in my life. 2021 and 2022 were nothing like 2018, 2019, and 2020. The new places, the new people, the new experiences...until I lived that life, I never could have imagined what was in store for me. 2021 and 2022 became some of the hardest and most challenging times in my life. Those years changed me like no others. Transcendence through the hard times led my mind to a space where I became capable of writing books.

I had both good and bad days; during the days depicted in the stories and during the times when I wrote the stories. Each affects the other. The things I've experienced have helped shape me into who I am. How I felt in those instances helped shape the outcome of those experiences. How I felt when I wrote became another influence on the way the past experiences were put into words. Everything, past and present, became fluid together in the creation process. I never considered that factor until I experienced it as I began the writing process.

Through my deal with myself back in 2018, I kept going. Having made good on that deal, I keep going. I have one more book left in this journey through a unique time period. I have one more book to lead me to the closure of that deal with myself. I'd debate on whether I would grow from this experience, or if this would just be one long suicide note. I've already grown, and I will continue to grow as I move forward.

The next book will be the culmination of transcendence to my true calling in life. As I write this now, I'm excited for the future. I'm writing this to close out this fourth book in preparation for the fifth. This postscript, originally planned for the end of the series, now serves another purpose. Originally set as closure, it now serves as transition to my most important piece of writing; one which I can now begin to write.

Just now, the idea came to me. I didn't know how I was going to proceed until I typed the final sentence of the last chapter of **2021: My Last Hope**. Now it all makes sense. I have a plan, and I have a vision for the fifth and final book in the series, sharing a name with the series itself. The name, important to me, was my thought back in 2018, when I made that original deal with myself; a deal with which I honestly surprise myself with each step closer to its realization.

Washed Away to Nothing with the Memories of Ghosts

A series of five books, written by: **Douglas Schnapp**

2018: My Last Hope
2019: My Last Hope
2020: My Last Hope
2021: My Last Hope

and coming soon, the final book in the series:

Washed Away to Nothing with the Memories of Ghosts

www.ingramcontent.com/pod-product-compliance
Lightning Source LLC
Chambersburg PA
CBHW060926040426
42445CB00011B/816